ᴆ ULLSTEIN

The Book

40 years of divided Germany have left their traces. The problems of growing together again bear witness to this. And yet even today it is hardly possible to make out where the Wall stood. There is good reason to make the effort to remember: the authors undertook a voyage into the past to events and scenes of action which outraged and shocked not only the people of Germany. The result is a vividly presented documentation that takes the reader through five eventful decades of German history.

The Authors

The Berliner Werner Sikorski (text), an experienced political reporter and commentator, headed up the political section of the BZ and the Berlin editorial staff of *DIE WELT AM SONNTAG*. He is now on the editorial staff of *Die Welt*. Rainer Laabs (picture editor) is in charge of the Ullstein documentation section and the library.

Werner Sikorski/Rainer Laabs

Checkpoint Charlie and the Wall

A Divided People Rebel

Ullstein

Welcome to our website:
www.ullstein-taschenbuch.de

Ullstein is a part of Ullstein Buchverlage GmbH.
6. edition 2004
© 2004 by Ullstein Buchverlage GmbH
© 2003 by Ullstein Heyne List GmbH & Co. KG
© 2001 by Econ Ullstein List Verlag GmbH & Co. KG, Berlin
© 1997 by Ullstein Buchverlage GmbH & Co. KG, Berlin
Originally published in Germany under the title:
Checkpoint Charlie und die Mauer – Ein geteiltes Volk wehrt sich
by Ullstein Buchverlage GmbH & Co. KG, Berlin
Translated from the German by George Bailey
Translation © 1998 by Ullstein Buchverlage GmbH Co. KG, Berlin
Cover design: Simone Fischer & Christof Berndt, Visuelle Kommunikation, Berlin
Cover photo courtesy of Archiv für Kunst und Geschichte, Berlin
All rights reserved
Printed in Germany
by Ebner & Spiegel, Ulm
ISBN 3-548-33237-4

Table of Contents

Foreword

For 28 years, two months and 27 days, Berlin was split into two parts. The closely guarded barricades which separated West Berlin from East Berlin and the surrounding state of Brandenburg were 155 kilometers long. 107 kilometers were of stone, the rest barbed wire or the walls of buildings which had survived the war.

Scarcely half a decade after the historic collapse of the Wall on November 9, 1989, little of it remains to be seen. Most of it was ground up into gravel and utilized to construct high-ways in the former German Democratic Republic. A few sections bearing the unique Wall graffiti were presented as gifts around the world. Years after the collapse, small fragments are still being sold to tourists as souvenirs.

Those same tourists frequently travel around Berlin asking: where was the Wall anyway? Where was "East" and where was "West"? And when they actually find a surviving piece of the Wall, they are "happy" and get their pictures taken.

It seems yesterday's tragedies are quickly forgotten. In 1996 a Berlin newspaper conducted a poll of youths who had been five years old when the Wall fell. The result: the chil-dren, now twelve years old, had hardly any recollections of the heart-rending events of November 1989.

Will the forgetfulness of the young be made even greater by the disinterest of the old? Quite a few West Berliners had made themselves comfortable in the Wall's shadow, creating an idyll for themselves which was destroyed in 1989. Now big city traffic rumbles again along the thoroughfares once closed off, and the meditative quiet of yesterday is now a thing of the past. A snapshot in northern Berlin: a section of the Wall was to be preserved there, but the protests were deafening. "We don't want to be reminded of the horrors of those days every time we look out the window" went the refrain. Other voices complained about the unrestricted influx of foreigners and the allegedly concomitant rise in the crime rate. Many persist in dividing the German population into "Ossis" and "Wessis". Some deplore the arrogance, the "know-it-all" attitude, and the triumphalism of the "Wessis", while others accuse the "Ossis" of ingratitude and feeling sorry for themselves.

What then became of the great, heartfelt excitement and compassion felt by one and all at the Wall's collapse? One speaks of the "Wall in one's head". Granted, that is only a slogan, but nonetheless one with a baleful origin. Years after the collapse of the Wall, people still speak of "over there", and when they go "over there" it is almost like a trip to a foreign country. Even in Berlin there is an invisible border: in the boroughs of former East Berlin, the residents prefer to read the newspapers published in their boroughs, and the same is true in old West Berlin. There is even a "marriage border": of the 16,383 marriages in Berlin in 1994, a mere 377 women native to East Berlin said "I do" to a "Wessi", and conversely only 185 West Berlin women married an "Ossi".

Years after the collapse of the Wall, politicians are trying to do battle against forgetfulness — more than a little late, in the opinion of critics. A discussion has begun: should the remaining sections of the Wall continue to deteriorate or should they be restored? Should the former course of the Wall be marked by metal strips set into the ground? Or will that which is said in various parts of the world about the Germans be proven correct, that they have an inadequate awareness of history?

From Germany to Germany

Walls have been built since man first learned to pile up stones. Cities surrounded themselves with them, and noblemen defended their keeps. It was almost always a matter of repelling attackers and guaranteeing people safety behind one's walls. The greatest bulwark in the world was built in China. Its construction was begun in 211 B.C. and it reached its final form in the fifteenth century. This structure measured 1,500 miles (2,450 kilometers) long.

And why was the Berlin Wall built? The Communist architects maintained that it was to protect the people living behind it, because after all NATO was just waiting to march their troops through the Brandenberg Gate with fifes and drums.

To offer people protection from aggression: the builders of the Berlin Wall were never able to support such a claim, despite the best efforts of their propagandists. The real reason for building the wall was plain for the whole world to see: its sole purpose was to stop the massive flow of refugees from East to West in Germany.

This goal dovetailed neatly with the interests of the Soviet Union. Its western outpost was not to spiral into a life-threatening crisis, nor should the empire erected by Stalin after the Second World War suffer any serious damage.

Apart from that, this emigration from one part of Germany to the other was a perpetual public relations fiasco for the socialist camp's pretensions of superiority to the West and its economic system. In 1949 alone, the year Bonn and East Berlin were constituted into two countries, 59,245 Germans moved from East to West. One year later it was already 197,788. The record was set in the year of the ruthlessly suppressed popular uprising of June 17, 1953, when 331,390 people left everything to go West. The five years remaining before the Wall would each see more than 200,000 departures westward.

According to official statistics, a total of 2,689,922 people fled to the west in the period from 1949–1961. The real number is probably significantly higher, as not a few simply moved in unofficially with family and friends, without running the gauntlet of the refugee bureaucracy.

Until the Wall, the trip from East to West was not likely to be dangerous. About half of all refugees chose the West Berlin route, because it was the most convenient. A subway or local train was all it took to reach the West. Those with lots of baggage would be sure to arouse suspicion and might not make it past the border authorities. Those convicted of intent to emigrate faced the legal consequences of "Flight from the Republic". This offence was treated as a criminal act punishable with up to three years in prison.

The refugees were housed in emergency camps, constructed expressly for that purpose in West Berlin and several other West German cities. In peak periods the refugee flow exceeded the capacity of the West Berlin camp, with its 3,000 beds, so often that supplementary emergency quarters had to be provided. In order to qualify for political refugee status, which carried the promise of economic assistance, one had to prove severe and independently verifiable political duress. Once this investigation was completed the refugees who had come to West Berlin were immediately flown to West Germany and allotted among the individual states.

Over the years the inexhaustible flow of refugees represented not only a unique loss of prestige for the East German regime, but also an enormous economic bloodletting: skilled workers from every field came West, but especially scientists, engineers, doctors, and senior managers. Most striking was the high percentage of well-educated young people between twenty and thirty years of age.

This development caused the East German regime to grow increasingly nervous. The magnetic attraction of West Berlin as the "showcase of freedom" was indescribable. To counteract this, the SED Socialist Party leadership under Walter Ulbricht struggled to obtain Russian approval of the idea of a blockade, initially without success as the Russians were not interested in new international complications.

By 1961, however, in light of the sheer number of refugees as well as bottlenecks in the economy, such a move appeared inevitable. On July 3–4 Ulbricht summoned the members of his party's central committee and invited the ambassadors from the eastern bloc countries. He confirmed the statistics on the refugees that had been published in the West as accurate, and hinted that East Germany might not be able to uphold her eastern bloc trade commitments by the end of the year. What was more, in his view a dangerous mood had arisen in the GDR, one which potentially could be exploited by NATO to incite a new popular rebellion like that of June 17, 1953.

Ulbricht's warnings alarmed Moscow. At a meeting of the Eastern bloc heads of state, held in Moscow from August 3–5, 1961, the East German ruler received unanimous approval of his plan to seal the approaches to the West. Immediately upon his return Ulbricht convened the members of his SED Politburo to inform them of the decision from Moscow. Under the tightest security, initial preparations were begun: the prepositioning of four divisions of the National People's Army within the borders of Berlin, fully equipped with transport machinery and material for the first provisional barricades. This deployment was militarily secured by the Soviet Union. The Soviet premier, Nikita Khrushchev, entrusted the command of the operation to 63-year-old Marshal Ivan S. Konjew, who in 1945 had taken part in the battle of Berlin. He had twenty Soviet divisions placed at his disposal.

Despite the tight security these preparations did not pass unnoticed in the West. To suspicious questions Konjew offered the friendly reply: "Gentlemen, you may be completely at ease." Nothing would be undertaken against West Berlin, and the existing rights granted the Western powers under the city's four-power status would not be infringed. Even in East Germany rumors circulated of an imminent blockade of West Berlin. These rumors precipitated large increases in the numbers of refugees, as the daily counts of refugees in early August showed: 2305, 1741, 1926, 1573.

Apparently in an effort to counteract the spreading rumors, Ulbricht called an international press conference in the "House of Ministers", to which 350 western journalists came. When Annemarie Doherr, the Berlin correspondent of the Frankfurter Rundschau asked with regard to the increasing rumors whether all the talk of the creation of a "Free City of West Berlin" meant that East Germany would now draw the national border at the Brandenburg Gate, he replied: "I interpret your question as follows: that there are people in West Germany who wish that we would mobilize the construction workers of East Berlin to build a wall, is that right? I am not aware that any such intention exists. The construction workers of our city are occupied chiefly with the construction of apartment buildings. No one has any intention of building a wall."

Contained in Ulbricht's answer was a Freudian slip: despite all the rumors, no one in the West had used the word "wall." Scarcely two months after this press conference, the preparations for building the wall were in full swing. During the night of August 13th, the barricades would go up. As so often throughout history, Sunday was chosen as the day to carry out the plan — a time when most people were at home and the responsible civil authorities were weekending at their country houses.

With the construction of the Wall the entire significance of a momentous decision was revealed: a decision that had been made in 1944, when the defeat of Germany was just a matter of time. On September 12 of that year, representatives

"No one has any intention of building a wall!", declared Walter Ulbricht on June 15, 1961 at an international press conference. In truth, round-the-clock preparations for the concretization of the border were already underway.

of the Soviet Union, the United States, and Great Britain met to draft the treaty that would divide defeated Germany into three parts. France would join in later as the fourth victorious power. In the "special Berlin sector", the Allies were all to be represented equally and were to create a so-called Kommandatura for the multilateral administration of the greater Berlin area.

All seemed harmonious, but the seeds of conflict had been sown. Shortly after the war, the Soviets disavowed that part of the agreement that declared Berlin a separate occupation zone, ignoring the fact that the end of the London Protocol reads in unmistakable black and white: "... with the exception of the Berlin Sector, for which a special form of occupation is foreseen." Despite this unequivocal statement, the Soviet Union continuously sought to dislodge the Western Allies from the city. The "Blockade" of 1948–49 saw the severing of all passenger and freight links that crossed the Soviet-occupied zone. The city was supplied with food and coal for almost a year by the Allies' airlift, with up to 927 flights a day. 1948 also witnessed the collapse of the multilateral administration, which led to Berlin's being governed by two magistrates. Ten years later Khrushchev demanded in an ultimatum a "Free City of West Berlin", which entailed the withdrawal of allied military forces. Another aspect of Soviet policy was the declaration of East Berlin as the capital of East Germany.

The Allies, however, remained in West Berlin, and they had the support of the overwhelming majority of the West Berlin population. The former United States Secretary of State, Henry Kissinger, spoke to this point in his "Memoirs: 1968–1973": "It has become abundantly clear that the freedom of Berlin paradoxically depended on the city's remaining militarily occupied. That was the only basis on which the United States and its allies could resist the pressure of the Soviet Union and East Germany, however anomalous that may have been for a generation after the end of the Second World War."

The political response of the Allies was the policy of "de-escalation", and the coming division of the city could not be prevented.

In the three years following Khrushchev's ultimatum, East Germany's internal contradictions grew considerably worse. The looming proximity of West Berlin — still freely accessible — acted politically and economically as the often-quoted "arrow in the flesh of Communism". To the consternation of the East German power brokers, the "economic miracle" of West Germany generated an unforeseen magnetic field. Emergency measures, including the suppression of the popular uprising of June 17, 1953, the collectivization of agriculture begun the previous year, restrictions on individual freedom of expression, the prosecution of political critics across the spectrum, and the everyday ordeals in an economy of scarcity all caused a growing refugee movement. Would East

14

Germany continue to suffer losses cutting so close to the bone, or stanch the flow by sealing the hatches to the West?

Berlin Divided

A reassuring communiqué from the West Berlin State Office for the Protection of the Constitution was introduced in the West Berlin Senate on Friday, the 11th of August, 1961: according to all available information, "no unusual events" were expected over the coming weekend. Reassuring, because the mass exodus out of East Germany had created a high-tension atmosphere. Over the last two days another 2,662 people had fled West. Then one of the Berlin newspapers appeared with the headline: "SED To Block Escape Routes".

That made the report that reached the duty captain at police headquarters at 1:54 a.m. on August 13th all the more disturbing: the train station at Gesundbrunnen, which was

The "heir apparent" in the Central Committee of the SED, Erich Honecker, was responsible for the smooth implementation of the Wall's construction.

Armed East German troops marched up to the Brandenburger Tor and blocked access to the most famous symbol of German unity.

The Wall's construction was supposedly a purely German affair, but fully-armed Soviet tanks, like those here on the Warschauer Brücke, were deployed throughout East Berlin.

Soldiers of the GDR's National People's Army (NVA) secured the Sector's borders at the corner of Elsen- and Heidelberger Straße between Neu Kölln and Treptow

situated in the French sector, reported that all trains had been stopped.

Over on the eastern side of the city secret preparations had long since been under way. Ulbricht's protegé Eric Honecker set up his command post for the coming hours and days at East Berlin's police headquarters, surrounded by an eight man staff. Every order that issued from this group was given by mouth in order to guarantee absolute security. The word "wall" was not to be mentioned to anyone. Soviet as well as East German army divisions were placed on alert.

Soon the reports began piling up: at 12:30 a.m. tanks and troops from the East German army had taken up positions on Unter den Linden, at 2:30 the thoroughfare at the Brandenburg Gate was blocked off. Not only here, but in multiple locations in East Berlin, including Alexanderplatz, Soviet tanks rolled into position. As dawn broke, the few early risers saw an astonishing thing: between East and West Berlin a barbed

Free special editions of the newspapers informed West Berlin residents about the events on August 13th. Many readers had slept right through the beginning of the construction early Sunday morning.

wire barrier had appeared. Border guards and motorized infantry units had been drawn up and were stopping all traffic between the two parts of the city.

By 6:00 a.m. it was clear to all observers: the intention was to divide the city. With the exception of the transit routes

A scene from August, 1961. It would be 28 years before these children could overrule the separation of Germany.

to West Germany, all 95 streets that led to West Berlin had been closed off. Only thirteen crosspoints remained open, but those were all heavily guarded. No East Berliner was allowed to pass, it was said, unless he had permission. At the same time, the Green Border between East and West Germany was fortified with barricades. The first ineffective protests began quickly among the West Berliners. In the east, it was clear that the escape routes would now be permanently closed off. With isolation staring them in the face, an estimated one thousand people tried to flee in panic.

At the corner of Bernauer- and Ackerstraßen, a car smashed through the provisional barricades. At Bethaniendamm a group of 16 people made it across. A father, his three-year-old son on his back, navigated the Landwehrkanal and made it safely to the western bank. Other refugees came by way of coal

Within days of the start of the Wall's construction, more than 300,000 Berliners gathered in front of the Schöneberger Rathaus to protest the division of their city and the protecting Powers' failure to react.

The then-Mayor, Willy Brandt, gave voice to the crowd's fears in no uncertain terms.

bunkers, through the canal network, or hidden in potato shipments.

Already on this August 13th a sense of astonished disappointment was widespread among the West Berlin population at the restraint with which the western Allies had greeted the blockade: would they tolerate this division of the city? Then-Mayor Willy Brandt publicly demanded "energetic steps". Chancellor Konrad Adenauer announced countermeasures. But neither politician nor population had yet in those hectic hours and days grasped what had been tacitly agreed upon among the Allies: they saw neither their responsibility to protect the West Berlin population nor their own rights in West Berlin in any way threatened. Although Brandt, before a crowd of more than 300,000 emotional West Berliners, demanded "more than words" from the American President, the attitude of the three western powers remained unper-

21

Particularly dramatic escape scenes occurred along Bernauer Straße in the Wedding district, where the front of the buildings formed the border. As 77-year-old Frieda Schultze tried to jump out of her window into the West on Sept. 24, 1961, People's Police officers and Stasi collaborators who had forced their way into her apartment tried to prevent her escape.

In the first days after the Wall was built, the doors of buildings fronting Bernauer Straße were sealed, but the windows of ground floor apartments had not yet been barricaded. Many took advantage of that fact to escape.

turbed: protests, yes — countermeasures, no. Neither British Prime Minister Harold Macmillan nor French President Charles de Gaulle felt obliged by events to interrupt their vacations. Under the rationale that "the Soviets were operating only in the eastern sector", the American government advisors recommended against any interference.

Unsettled by the increasingly explosive situation, the politicians and people needed some time before they could comprehend this new geopolitical constellation. Comprehension was made more difficult by events which grew more dramatic every day. At the barricades which Ulbricht had called an "antifascist freedom boundary", each day brought spectacular escape attempts. Near the Thuringian city of Sonneberg 70 people clambered over the barbed wire. Near Har-

On Sept. 22, 1961, residents of No. 7 Bernauer Straße escaped by throwing themselves from the fifth floor into a safety net spread below by the West Berlin Fire Department.

Many people who lived directly along the Wall simply had to move out immediately.

leshausen a 21-year-old junior officer in the border guard outfoxed his comrades and sped across the wire barricade on a motorcycle. In Berlin eight people, including four children, crashed through the barriers in a truck. At 110 Harzer Straße, where the houses belonged to the East but the fronting streets to the West, a 24 year-old-man lowered himself out of his apartment window.

Many successful attempts, but many tragedies too: on Bernauer Straße, where again the buildings were the East's but the streets the West's, 58-year-old Ida Seikmann died of the injuries she sustained attempting to jump into a safety net stretched below by the West Berlin Fire Department. In response to this and other escape attempts the East German government bricked up all the windows in the lower floors of these buildings, and the occupants were forcibly relocated.

At the Teltower Canal, a 30-year-old man was shot dead as he attempted to reach the other shore. He was the third casualty of those early days. The same fate awaited another man, again in the Teltower Canal. In the Baltic Sea a group of twelve sailors attempted to commandeer the ship "Seebad Binz", in order to make for a West German port. Their attempt failed, and they were later punished with jail sentences of up to five years. Three Coast Guardsmen had better luck: while on patrol they overpowered their crewmates and succeeded in reaching the West German port of Travemünde. A camera-

The Berliners greeted U. S. reinforcements with cheers as they arrived at control point Dreilinden.

man from West Berlin was arrested while attempting to get his fiancée out of East Berlin, and sentenced to five years in prison. In another case against three East Berliners accused of attempting to escape together, jail terms of up to three and one half years were handed down.

Ten days after the barricades appeared Adenauer finally arrived in the city. His absence had contributed heavily to the disenchantment among the West Berlin population. The Chancellor had feared — at least according to his advisors — that the precarious situation would only be exacerbated by his presence, and he wanted to spare the Allies that eventuality. Washington too wanted to calm the fears which by then had changed to outrage, and dispatched Vice President Lyndon B. Johnson to Berlin. The West Berliners, who in those days were thankful for any gesture, prepared an enthusiastic reception for him — hundreds of thousands of people swarmed into the streets. Johnson delivered a message from President John F. Kennedy: West Berlin's freedom and free access to

A picture of Kremmener Straße, which illustrates the insane logic of Berlin's division.

East Berlin for the western powers were guaranteed. At the same time a motorized battalion of 1,500 men was sent across East Germany along the access routes to West Berlin to strengthen the garrison there — a symbolic step, intended to strengthen the psychological powers of resistance in West Berlin. Lastly, General Lucius Clay arrived in the city as President Kennedy's personal representative. He was well known for his hard nosed attitude toward the Communists. In 1948, in response to the Soviet blockade, Clay had pushed the implementation of the airlift through the White House. Nevertheless it became clearer with each passing week that the Allies had reconciled themselves to the division of Berlin.

Even the Peace of the Dead Was Dishonored

The barricades were systematically reinforced around the clock. Walls of concrete block soon appeared in place of the

Shortly after the first barricades were put up, the "Anti-Fascist Defensive Wall" was built behind plywood screens. In the background one can see the Reichstag Building.

barbed wire. The civilian masons were closely guarded by soldiers. Only married workers were allowed on site, as the regime feared that unmarried people would flee.

Anything that stood in the way of this hectic reinforcement was ruthlessly shoved aside. A number of Berlin cemeteries were situated along the newly leveled border zone, many of them dating back a hundred years. Most of the headstones were unfeelingly removed to guarantee a clear field of fire. No one took the trouble to rebury the dead first. Those cemeteries which survived the bulldozers could only be visited with special permission. The cemetery of the catholic parish of St. Hedwig, at the corner of Liesen- and Chauseestraße, which in 1777 was the first catholic burial ground established in Berlin, was virtually demolished during the construction of the Wall. In the death strip along the Wall was also the cemetery of the French Reformed congregation, in which was buried Theodore Fontane, the author or "Mark Brandenburg". The grounds were closed from 1961 until 1984 and thereafter

How must this construction worker have felt as he walled himself in while being guarded by border troops at the intersection of Bernauer- and Schwedter Straße?

The first watchtower was erected by the People's Police on Lohmüh-lenplatz.

WER UNS
ANGREIFT
WIRD
VERNICHTET

The propaganda surrounding the construction of the Wall left little room for doubt. Here tank traps were built along Niederkirchnerstraße at the "House of Ministers", which would later become the "Trusteeship Center"

Those who walled in the living had no respect for the peace of the dead: the transfer of remains at the Sophienfriedhof on Bernauer Straße during the modernization of the Wall in 1967.

could be visited only with special permission. Every step of the infrequent visitors was closely watched from nearby guard towers. The most horrible fate befell the Veterans Cemetery on Scharnhorststraße, which was established in 1784. It had been a monument to German and Prussian history from time immemorial. There rested generals, ministers of war, and other figures of note. Names such as Scharnhorst, Winterfeld, Lützow, Boyen, Schlieffen, Witzleben, and many others were engraved on headstones and monuments carved by artists like Friedrich Schinkel and Christian Daniel Rauch. Three fields of graves were completely leveled in the first weeks, and the rest of the cemetery could be visited only with a special pass. Between the monuments signs were posted with the warnings "Caution: Firearms In Use!" and "Photography Forbidden!"

The grievous total: of the 3,000 graves that existed before the Wall, only 230 could be found after it fell. After the collapse of Communism the citizens of the city passed a referendum, which will attempt to save what can be saved. Along with the cemeteries, a church also fell victim to the Wall's construction: the Protestant Church of the Reconciliation (Versöhnungskirche), which straddled the border between the boroughs of Mitte (East) and Stadtmitte (West), was cut off from its congregation by the establishment of the death strip. For years the church, dedicated in 1894, stood in a no-man's-land.

The ironically-named Protestant (evangelische) "Church of the Reconciliation" was levelled on Jan. 28, 1985 to create a clear field of fire.

In January 1985, during the course of "renovations" to the border strip, it was dynamited by the East Berlin authorities. In the seventh year after the demolition of the Wall, the congregation decided to build a new center of worship on the old site, complete with chapel and a memorial.

Beneath the Death Strip

Among the peculiarities of the divided city was the fact that the West German trains and subways ran beneath the death strip. A total of fifteen stations in the Soviet sector were shut down and access to them denied to the East Berlin public. The West Berlin trains and subways were allowed to pass through them at a walking pace and so preserved the major north-south connections in the city. This concession was a lucrative one for the eastern side: in the beginning it received

Some West Berlin subway tracks passed beneath areas of East Berlin. Strongly guarded shut-down ghost stations like this one at Potsdamer Platz had to be passed through at walking speed.

2.8 million marks a year from the West Berlin transit authorities, which climbed to six million by the end of the 1980's.

The journey under the death strip was a spooky affair: the train stations were eclipsed in a gloomy half-light. At each station two guard posts had the task of ensuring that no trespassing East Germans tried to leap onto the slowly moving trains. But the GDR had also placed physical obstacles in this path: every entrance to these stations was either walled up or, as at Potsdamer Platz, completely demolished. Only the Friedrichstraße station remained open. Here in accordance with the terms of the Passport Convention West Berlin visitors could disembark, pass through the controls, and cross into East Berlin.

As most of the soldiers stationed in the closed stations did not come from East Berlin, a special orientation course had been provided for them. Thus, in East Berlin's Schwarzkopfstraße subway station, an arrow with the word "Enemy" pointed in the direction of the Wedding station, which lay in the French sector. On a second arrow, pointing toward the Stadtmitte station in the Soviet sector, was the word "Friend". What was more, the tracks at the subterranean border were strongly barricaded. A system of iron bars and illuminated barriers was intended to prevent any attempts to escape. In addition, acoustic sensors were set into the ground, which sounded the alarm if disturbed.

In his book "Forty Years" (published by S. Fisher), the writer Günter de Bruyn described the attempts of many Berliners not to fall prey to longing for the West, but to steel themselves against this divided state of affairs so as to avoid debilitating anguish. That proved impossible in the case of the darkened stations: "... and when every five minutes one heard the subway trains rumbling by under the pavement from West to West, sooner or later one would have to stop thinking, oh to be able to go along, to Tegel or Neukölln. To survive living in a cage, one had to pretend that the cage didn't exist."

In addition all the abandoned stations were excised from the maps of the day. In the same way, on most maps West Berlin was depicted as a large white blotch. In the years after the collapse, reminders of the "time of troubles" are scarcely to be seen. Traffic flows as though nothing had happened, and growing children have no recollection of that time.

From West Berlin to West Berlin Via Footpath

"Surreal" is the only way to describe the complications which the 150 residents of the enclave of Steinstücken had to face. The 30 acre enclave had been cut off from its home county when the Wall was built. If the residents wanted to get there, they had to traverse a 1200-yard-long footpath. Nonresident visitors were not allowed. Along the way to Zehlendorf the residents of Steinstücken had to pass two checkpoints, where even schoolchildren had to open their satchels. In the aftermath of the Wall's appearance, the fate of the enclave seemed to hang from a silken thread — would East Germany take the risk of simply annexing the enclave?

On September 21 the Americans made their position unmistakably clear: General Clay flew to Steinstücken in a military helicopter and thus underscored West Berlin's claim to the enclave. From then on three U. S. soldiers were posted in Steinstücken as a permanent guard. They stayed in constant contact with headquarters via radio. Every three or four days a U. S. helicopter would land to relieve the personnel and deliver supplies.

The worst ended for the Steinstücken residents with the Four Power Agreement of June 3, 1972. Unrestricted access to visitors was secured by a 20-yard-wide alley. The enclave remained completely cut off from the East German sector.

Today the erstwhile helicopter landing pad is the site of a memorial from the thankful population. The ceremonies mark-

Completely normal insanity in the divided city: A British armored vehicle had to accompany young Erwin Schabe from the Eiskeller enclave to Spandau every day on his way to school.

Among the curiosities of the borderline was the so-called "Duckbill" in Hermsdorf, where a neatly walled-off part of the "East" stuck out into West Berlin.

Only a narrow lane led to Steinstücken, until in the wake of the "De-Escalation Measures" a broader street was dedicated on August 30, 1972, by the then-Lord Mayor Klaus Schütz.

ing the departure of the Allies in July 1994 were attended by a number of former helicopter pilots. For the last time a type UH1H helicopter landed — reminding Steinstücken residents of their darkest period.

The Palace of Tears

At the Friedrichstraße train station, on a onetime parking lot, stood the so-called Palace of Tears. The building, which resembled a huge barracks of steel and glass, was erected eleven months after the Wall in order to move the customs and control process for disembarking West German visitors out of the train station. It quickly earned the nickname "Palace of Tears" because of the parting scenes which were played out before its entrance doors between East Berliners and their friends and relatives from the West.

The border near Lübars. In 1969 the old wooden watchtower was re-placed by a new one of precast concrete segments. Even that was a form of prefabricated building.

The moment a West German visitor stepped into the Fried-richstraße intercity train station, a leaflet would be pressed into his or her hands: "Dear Traveler! We welcome you to the German Democratic Republic and wish you a pleasant stay. We take this opportunity to inform you of several regu-lations which must be observed while entering and leaving and while you are in the German Democratic Republic in-cluding its capital, democratic Berlin."

Visitors from West Berlin and West Germany had to run a gauntlet that many found degrading. Luggage was thoroughly searched, even cigarette boxes were opened and checked.

Customs collected the obligatory fees, payable in West German currency, and stamped the official stamps. East German currency could not be brought in or out. Any expenses had to be met by exchanging western currency for eastern at the official 1:1 rate, an extra morsel for perennially cash-starved East Germany.

After the collapse of the Wall a cabaret was opened in the Palace of Tears, and concerts were given as well. Old signs with inscriptions like "Departure [West] Berlin Citizens" and "Passport Control for Arriving Citizens of West Berlin, West Germany and Other Countries Via Platform B" still served as reminders of bygone days.

West German citizens attempting to drive from East to West Berlin had to use one of the two official crosspoints, at Prinzenstrasse or the Bornholmer Bridge. West Berliners could use the Prinzenstrasse crossing and ones at Oberbaumbrücke, Chausseestraße, and Sonnenallee as well. Probably the most famous crossing, "Checkpoint Charlie" was reserved for foreigners.

At every barricade as a rule three border guards were on duty. They checked one's papers, the bar was raised, and then the real control process began. The occupants of every car had to get out and go into the control barracks to show their papers again, which were closely examined by the border guards. During periods of peak traffic it often came to lengthy delays. Those coming from East Berlin were examined equally closely. The trunks of cars had to be opened — a refugee could be hiding there. And not only there — perhaps underneath in the frame of the chassis too. To check this, a mirror on wheels was rolled under the car. Things could really get backed up when West Berliners trying to move to West Germany appeared in their unsealed moving vans at the checkpoints. Any books among the luggage had to be individually unpacked, and titles banned in the Democratic Republic of Germany were often confiscated.

Escape in the Trunk

Actually, despite the efficiency of the border and control procedures, there was one escape possibility that East Germany could never completely control — escape in the trunk. This opportunity saw courageous idealists quickly followed by rash businessmen and adventurers. Networks similar to those among secret service agencies sprang up, based in private apartments. There one could find informants who recruited East Germans looking to emigrate and daring helpmates with West German passports who had the nerve to engage in conspiratorial activity in the East Berlin sector. Matching the supply with the demand was extremely dangerous, but just as lucrative. Once the finances were taken care of, the refugee would be delivered to a sparsely populated suburb of East Berlin and hidden in the trunk of a car. Then the journey to West Germany began along the transit route. That kind of help in escaping could easily cost up to 15,000 U. S. dollars. Seemingly unabashed, even running thinly-disguised advertisements in the newspapers, the "Aramco Corporation" was the brainchild of a man named Hans Ulrich Lenzlinger, and operated out of Zurich. Sixteen escape experts worked for him, most of them young people with no particular profession, looking for adventure and a lucrative payoff. The price for their help was 20–25,000 marks. Families got group discounts. Lenzlinger credibly claimed that 400 East German citizens had been smuggled into the west by this operation. A million mark business, when one considers the asking prices.

It is not surprising that such a bold operator in escape assistance soon fell into the toils of the East German state security services. Their First Chief Directorate included death squads operating in the West who kidnapped or liquidated those designated as East Germany's most dangerous enemies. So it was no great surprise when Lenzlinger was found shot to death in his villa. The case was never solved.

One other form of human smuggling evolved in East Berlin. The operators of this escape route were almost impossible for the state security services to catch. They were diplomats, in principal poorly paid low-ranking delegates from the Third World. In their role as smugglers these individuals exploited the fact that as diplomats they could not be searched at the border. This escape channel was routed chiefly through Checkpoint Charlie, which was after all reserved for foreigners. Here too the stakes ran to five figures. It is difficult to estimate how many people reached the West this way. Those familiar with conditions at the time estimate several thousand. The East German authorities knew exactly what was happening, but had to bite their tongues. In only one case did they track down an accredited diplomat. It happened that the culprit turned out to be the chief of the embassy of a "socialist brotherland". The case involved the Cuban ambassador, Mauro Garcia Triana. The senior diplomat had brought out two women in exchange for a smuggler's fee of 50,000 D-marks. He was betrayed from within his own ranks and had to leave the GDR. Whether a criminal court was waiting for him at home is not known.

People smuggling was not the only business that flourished at Checkpoint Charlie. There were prominent gourmet food concerns in West Berlin which satisfied their demand for Russian caviar by means of shipments smuggled through Checkpoint Charlie. Invariably these deliveries involved diplomats. Not only caviar, but also valuable antiques, Russian icons, regimental plate from the czar's army, and silver were spirited into the West this way.

In contrast to the trade in humans, where West German Customs would pretend to look the other way, they would investigate every lead in cases where goods were involved. That was how a diplomat from Guinea's embassy fell into their hands, with antiques originating in Poland in his possession. An attaché from the same country was caught in his Audi 100 with 20,000 untaxed cigarettes. Diplomats from Mali's embassy brought five icons and a silver plate worth 80,000 marks into West Berlin. The record was probably set by two wives of African delegates accredited in Moscow. Believe it or not, they were caught with 65 icons, 70 pounds of caviar, and about one hundred valuable silver coins. Nevertheless West German Customs saw only the tip of the iceberg. And as long as that was the case, the smuggling business flourished for more than three decades. The diplomatic pipeline, through which a steady stream of people and goods flowed, was the only way out, with one exception that was open only to a few privileged individuals: official representatives were allowed into the West on official business and could take advantage of the opportunity and simply fail to return. To be sure, the regime was careful to allow only married people to undertake such journeys.

The Order to Shoot

Reinforcements of the security installations went forward without pause. Starting in 1975, the "Fourth Generation Wall" was built, known as "Border Wall 75" in eastern officialese. It stood twelve feet tall, and each of its segments was four feet wide. The wall was six inches thick. Each segment was buttressed five feet deep in the earth so that breakthroughs by main force were impossible even with the heaviest vehicles. With this renovation the Wall reached its final form.

In Berlin approximately 45.000 of these segments were installed. Each of these cost 359 East German marks to manufacture. The material used was ferro-concrete to which was added granules of agate. Before the collapse of the Wall there were pieces of earlier incarnations to be found throughout Berlin, including stone blocks, barbed wire, or concrete slabs festooned with broken glass or more wire.

The constantly "modernized" border was from the beginning the scene of indiscriminate shootings. Nevertheless, the

The construction engineers were at work practically around the clock on the construction of the Wall. Even as early as November of 1961, the first generation Wall on Kreuzberg's Zimmerstraße was being reinforced by a second.

View of the death strip and the Wall in the Mitte district of Berlin (the middle of Berlin). In the background is the Church of St. Thomas on Bethaniendamm in Kreuzberg.

existence of the often mentioned and widely criticized order to open fire was steadfastly denied by the Communist propagandists. Even Ulbricht, ousted as party leader in 1971, spoke of a Western "propaganda canard", and his successor Honecker repeatedly ridiculed the "alleged order to shoot". True it was, according to Honecker, that East Germany "protected its borders like any country in the world". Even after the Wall fell, leading functionaries of that era denied the existence of any orders to shoot.

This was contradicted by the secret orders of the East German leadership which were found after 1989. Thus it was established in directive number GVSTgb/Nr. 1/277/54 that as early as 1954, or seven years before the construction of the Wall, border guards were to fire their weapons aimed at illegal trespassers who disregarded orders to halt. Four years later, in Duty Directive DV III/2 dated September 1958, the order to fire at the refugees was to be given if there "was no other possibility of effecting the arrest through other approved means".

By September 20, 1961, the early weeks of the blockade had witnessed 216 violent breakthroughs involving 417 people, and Honecker summoned the leadership of the border guard: every attempt to break through would henceforth be stopped with lethal force. Refugees were to be fired on instantly if there was no chance of their arrest.

In the 1970's East Germany was at increasing pains to be recognized by the non-Communist world. That was Honecker's motive in signing the "International Convention on Human and Political Rights". In Article 12 therein was stated that "Every person had the right to leave any country, including his own." Taken literally, this passage would guarantee the right of every East German citizen to emigrate to the western portion of Germany. Only six months later, however, during a session of the "National Defense Council" in Strausberg examining the "State of the National Border", Honecker modified the instructions of the border units:

Again and again people tried to break through the Wall by force in the first years of the division. Here a successful attempt was made in April 1963 at Neu Kölln's Elsenstraße.

- The inviolability of the border of East Germany remains as always of paramount importance.
- It must be emphasized that attempts to breach the border will not be tolerated.
- In every case an open field of fire is to be maintained.
- As always in the case of attempts to breach the border fire-arms are to be used ruthlessly, and those comrades who have successfully used their weapons are to be commended.

Even before these amended orders of Honecker's, commendations had been in store for comrades who had prevented escape attempts with their firearms in the form of medals, extra leave, gifts, and cash bonuses. For the arrest of refugees, depending on one's rank, one could expect bonuses from 150 to 1,000 marks. The flip side of the coin: if in the

This attempt to crash through failed. It is not known even today how many escape attempts ended in a hail of border guard bullets.

pursuit of refugees it could be proven that border guards had intentionally shot to miss, they faced severe penalties — sentences of up to five years in a labor camp were well known.

The bullet-riddled corpses of refugees which could not be identified were cremated in the East Berlin crematorium Baumschulenweg. The relatives of successfully identified victims were allowed on request to hold a very quiet, supervised funeral service. When former co-workers attended such a service for someone who had been shot whilst trying to escape, the local SED party organized a campaign at the participants place of employment, reviling them as "provocateurs".

There is an intermediate Western statistic from the year 1986, according to which the use of weapons was proven in at least 1,638 instances, during which the arrests of 3,139 persons had been observed. The actual numbers, including the years up to the collapse of the wall, could well be significantly higher.

After the collapse of the Wall, former border guards suspected of shooting refugees were brought to trial by the Berlin justice authorities. According to statements by Berlin Justice Senator Lore-Maria Peschel-Gutzeit (SPD) in June of 1996, up to that time 40 sentences had been passed, most of them suspended sentences with probation. The verdict was "not guilty" in 20 cases.

But it was not just the little fish who should be brought before the court, but the big fish as well — those who bore the responsibility. Proceedings were begun against a number of them, including Honecker's successor Egon Krenz and SED Politburo members Horst Dohlus, Erich Mückenberger, Günter Schabowski, Günther Kleiber, and Kurt Hager. The defense attorneys went to great lengths to win dismissal of the charges. They presented a letter to the court from Soviet Marshal Victor Kulikov, who was the Supreme Commander of the combined Warsaw Pact forces from 1976–1989. He asserted that East Germany had never been politically or militarily sovereign, something their propaganda would never admit. In his letter the Marshal stressed that all the orders concerning the wall and border areas issued by responsible individuals in East Germany were not to be seen as autonomous. The highest echelons of the East German People's Army had been in daily contact with their Soviet counterparts. Every order down to "engineering and technical aspects of the border" were either issued or approved by the Soviet authorities.

In contrast to the five men accused with him, Günter Schabowski, the former editor-in-chief of the SED party organ "Neues Deutschland" and subsequent leader of the East Berlin party apparatus, was under no illusions regarding the problematic of right and wrong. He confessed to his moral culpability, but rejected being subsequently convicted of having masterminded the murders:

"Our messianic claim for the future of knowing how to create a Paradise of Righteousness must in view of the collapse accept the verdict of a stillborn reality." He expressed "guilt and shame" because of the people who had lost their lives on the wall and the wire. Schabowski confirmed what Kulikov's letter had told the court: "The construction of the Wall was impossible without the rationale, influence, and approval of Moscow, no matter how enthusiastically the East Germans Communists took up the cause."

Nevertheless Honecker's successor Egon Krenz was sentenced at the end of August 1997 to six and a half years imprisonment on charges involving three cases of manslaughter under his authorization. Likewise members of the SED-Politbüro, Günter Schabowski and Günther Kleiber, were sentenced to three years imprisonment each.

A Thousand Dogs On Patrol

In the hinterlands the usual barriers of walls and barbed wire were enhanced through the use of dogs. The state police maintained a dog training facility in Lobetal, which was in Barnim County thirty miles north by northeast of Berlin. There police dogs were trained for both the Stasi (secret police, short for Staatssicherheitsdienst) and the border guards. Every border regiment had its own units dedicated to police watchdog work. Dog-run cables, known in bureaucratese as the "TGL-Standard Model with Windproof Kennel", were installed along the intra-German border and even at times in Berlin's inner city. Each run consisted of a cable strung between man-high posts, which depending on the terrain could be up to 100 meters long. The dogs were attached to ten foot leads (attached to the cable with a pulley), and were trained to at-

At many locations within the city limits, as here in the St.-Hedwig-Friedhof on Liesenstraße, dogs were deployed on cable-runs for many years in the effort to secure the border.

tack intruders. In 1989 almost 1,000 dogs were in service along the length of the border.

Self-Firing Weapons and Mines

In contrast to Berlin no continuous wall was ever built along the entire 1,381 kilometer long border. Most of the inhabitants of the border strip were relocated in 1961 under Operation Cornflower. It worked as follows: the victims were given only a few hours in which to pack a part of their belongings. Then they were transported to areas far from the border. The majority of these forced relocations took place in Thuringia, the state with the longest border with the West German states of Niedersachsen, Hesse, and Bavaria. The victims' furniture was usually confiscated. People who were politically "reliable" were allowed to stay, but even they had to endure strict supervision and controls.

Wire fences, searchlights, motorcycle patrols, a system of bunkers and a total of 655 watchtowers were meant to make any escape attempt impossible. The results, however, were far from what the East German government had expected. Numerous successful escape attempts made the leadership tense. Under these circumstances the regime hit upon the idea of making the border less permeable through mines and self-firing weapons activated by trip-wires. By 1963 the East German defense minister could report to the SED Politburo that 4,526 mines, type PCMS-2, and 207,516 type PMD-6 had been laid. The type SM-70 self-firing weapon, which was installed beginning in early 1971, had a particularly gruesome effect. They were mounted at various heights along the new ten-foot-high expanded metal fencing of the "501 Barrier". Any disturbance set them off instantly, resulting in hideous wounds. One example among many: on April 1, 1981, the 21-year-old roofer Henry Leuschner and his friend Peter Dietz tried to relocate across the border zone in the vicinity of

Along the border between the GDR and West Germany, but not in and around Berlin, the notorious Self-Firing-Weapons were installed. Pictured is Model "SM-70", which can be seen in the "Haus am Checkpoint Charlie".

Plauen and in so doing set off the self-firing weapons. Peter Dietz suffered eight gunshot wounds, Henry Leuschner a total of 22. One bullet penetrated his chest, one grazed his head, another severed the artery under his arm, and several struck his calf. While Dietz was able to escape, the seriously wounded Leuschner was arrested. After his recovery, he was sentenced to a term of 21 months in prison, and ultimately deported to the West in 1983. The gruesome weapons quickly aroused towering indignation in the West. Honecker tried to deny the existence of the type SM-70. He characterized the Western protests as pure duplicity. According to him, these devices, dubbed "Death Machines" in the West, didn't even exist. This categorical denial motivated Michael Gartenschläger, a 32-year-old civil rights activist living in the West, to provide public proof of the existence of the SM-70. He had already succeeded in dismantling one of the devices under cover of darkness and delivering it to the Hamburg news weekly "Der Spiegel" as evidence. Now he set out to acquire another of the devices, in order to mount it in the street in front of the East German Permanent Mission in Bonn.

What Gartenschläger didn't know was that betrayal was in the works. There was a spy from the East German secret police in his neighborhood. When, during the night of May 1, 1976, he and two friends from Hamburg broke into the border zone at Border Post 231 east of Bröthen in Schleswig-Holstein, he was already expected. Several sharpshooters waiting in ambush opened fire without warning. Gartenschläger collapsed seriously hit. As both his friends escaped, he bled to death. His body was taken to Schwerin by East German border guards and there buried in an unknown grave.

The drama in Bröthen intensified Western protests. These were increasingly unpleasant for East Germany, as it was then intensifying its efforts to achieve international recognition and was under pressure to prove the sincerity of its policy of détente. As a result, after 1984 the self-firing weapons were dismantled and the mines were cleared, a decision influenced in no small measure by guaranteed multi-million mark credits from West Germany. Both projects were declared complete in 1985, which was true in the case of the self-firing weapons. For years after the Wall's collapse, minesweepers searched for mines, and continued to find them. According to statistics published by the Berlin group "Arbeitsgemeinschaft August 13", at least 39 refugees lost their lives to the mines.

Four days of Brinkmanship at Friedrichstraße

It has widely been forgotten how tense the geopolitical confrontation at the Wall became in October of 1961. The tension grew very quickly, but quietly died when the Eastern side gave up its attempt to restrict the Western powers' access to the Soviet sector. It began on the evening of October 22nd: the American envoy Allan Lightner planned to drive through Checkpoint Charlie with his wife to take in an opera, when unexpectedly and in violation of the rules he was ordered to produce his identity papers by the East German border guards. This was an unprecedented event, because allied personnel from all four powers were allowed free access throughout Berlin. Naturally the American envoy refused. He demanded in vain to speak to a Soviet officer. The U. S. State Department appeared close to accepting the new regulation, which was no doubt inspired by the Soviet Union. However, Kennedy's plenipotentiary General Clay immediately sent a warning to the President: if this revision of the rules was allowed to stand, then control of the transit routes as well would quickly fall into East German hands. Such a restriction of allied rights must not be accepted.

Washington agreed with Clay. When Clay learned that the Soviets had drawn up tanks on Potsdamer Platz, he sprang into action: at 8:30 a. m. on October 25th, a column of U. S.

Border control station at Checkpoint Charlie on Freiedrichstraße between the districts of Kreuzberg and Mitte in the year 1969.

armored vehicles and jeeps filled with combat-ready soldiers rolled up to Checkpoint Charlie. An American official held discussions with a Russian official, without success. At 10:45 a.m., two American civil servants in an official vehicle drove up to the toll-bar accompanied by a dozen U.S. soldiers with weapons loaded and bayonets fixed. The convoy passed through, entered the Soviet sector, and returned after four minutes. At 2:15 p.m., however, an American bus filled with soldiers and civilian personnel was again halted at the checkpoint. The Americans refused to produce their identification, and were then refused entry. In the meantime, the Americans had positioned a number of heavy tanks on Friedrichstraße. Over the next several hours the Soviets reacted by amassing thirty tanks, most of them T-54 s.

An explosive situation: 16 years after the end of the war the

Russian and American tanks confronted each other at point-blank range at Checkpoint Charlie. Perhaps the most dangerous situation in the history of the divided city.

two world superpowers and former allies faced each other at gunpoint, which laid to rest any Soviet claims regarding the alleged complete autonomy of the Democratic Republic of Germany. In alarm, worry, and fear, the world watched Checkpoint Charlie. There were even fears of a third world war. Even Albert Speer, Adolf Hitler's erstwhile Reichsminister, noticed the confrontation from the Spandau Prison run by the four powers for war criminals where he was serving his twenty year sentence.

In his "Spandau Diaries" (published by Propyläen), he described the events: "According to all accounts, we stood at the brink of war; in the prison dining hall, however, the opponents gathered together every few days and drank each other's health."

The situation defused itself with surprising speed. Khrushchev abruptly ordered the recall of his tanks. The Soviet party leader had been kept fully informed at all times about the situation. Had he been influenced by the Americans' firmness? In private circles he later gave this explanation for backing down: "Every child knows that tanks either move forward or backward. Had the tanks gone forward, it would have meant war, if they went back, it meant peace. Berlin had no importance for us, and therefore I ordered our tanks to withdraw."

In July-August 1961 he had been right in his calculation that the Western powers would make their peace with the building of the Wall, if only their rights to all Berlin were not infringed. This time too the Kremlin leader had calculated correctly, and as a result he quietly terminated the maneuver: at 9:45 a.m. on the 28th of October, the fourth day of the confrontation, the Soviet tanks were withdrawn. They would remain in the city limits for some time, but that was mostly a matter of saving face. The threatened major crisis was defused. A compromise of sorts had been reached: the Western powers agreed that in the future Allied personnel in civilian clothes would display their passports by holding them up to the windows of their vehicles — in effect a visual checkpoint, no more thorough search was permitted.

General Clay's efforts on behalf of the city did not pass unrecognized: he is the only person to have a street named for him in west Berlin while still living.

A Time for Dying: Peter Fechter

Barely a year after the confrontation between the tanks at Checkpoint Charlie, another incident caught the attention of the German public. In front of hundreds of horrified onlookers 18-year-old Peter Fechter died in anguish on the death strip not far from Checkpoint Charlie.

Together with his co-worker Helmut Kulbeik, also 18, the apprentice mason planned his escape. A resident of East Berlin's Weissensee district, he wanted to move in with a sister living in West Berlin, whom he had last seen shortly before the Wall went up. Fechter and his partner had reconnoitered a section along Zimmerstraße, only a few dozen meters from the foreigners' crosspoint Checkpoint Charlie, as ideal for their attempt.

Around noon on the 17 of August, 1962, they made their bid for freedom. They climbed the first barbed wire fence unseen. As they raced across the last few meters to the Wall, they were discovered and shot after ignoring orders to halt. As an investigation begun one year after the collapse of the Wall would later show, two border guards had fired a total of 21 shots at the two refugees. Although his co-worker clambered over the wall uninjured, Peter Fechter was struck a number of times in the back and abdomen. Seriously wounded, he lay on the ground a few yards short of the Wall.

Hundreds of West Berlin citizens quickly found themselves at the scene of a drama. At the top of their lungs they chanted demands at the eastern border guards as well as the American soldiers to help the wounded man. Nothing happened.

Peter Fechter shortly before 1960. A few years later he would become the most famous victim of the murderers at the Wall.

August 17, 1962: Peter Fechter was hit twice in the lungs and once in the stomach. He bled to death in agony right behind the Wall on Zimmerstraße in Kreuzberg.

Fechter's bloodstained body is removed. No picture could show more clearly the brutality of the GDR regime.

The U. S. soldiers could not legally intervene, and the eastern guards were supposedly waiting for higher orders. First aid kits thrown over the Wall were of no use to the bleeding man, who was already at the point of death. It was not until three o'clock in the afternoon that Fechter's dead body was removed by border guards and taken to a military hospital. The autopsy results were later shredded by the authorities. A simple memorial cross on Zimmerstraße remains a reminder of the lonely passing of Peter Fechter. The border guards involved were, as usual, rewarded with cash bonuses.

Three Corridors, Each 32 Kilometers Wide

Fortunately, Western fears that the Soviet Union would cause geopolitical complications by disrupting air travel to Berlin proved groundless. Aside from a few minor incidents, the three air corridors proved themselves reliable travel routes over the decades, especially to those people who had reason to fear persecution from the GDR. It was not just a matter of political safety — the corridors were very safe travel-wise as well. In 40 years not a single accident of consequence was recorded. 1971 was the record year, with 6,121,406 passengers carried. In 1989, the year before the collapse, the total was still 5,951,185.

This air traffic, which could be conducted only by companies from the Western powers, had its origin in the Air-Corridor Agreement of November 30, 1945. It accorded the three Western powers the air routes Berlin-Hamburg, Berlin-Bückeburg, and Berlin-Frankfurt am Main. Each of these corridors was 32 kilometers wide. In addition, an "Air Control Zone Berlin" was created, which, centered on the Allies' air traffic control center in Schöneberg, encompassed a radius of 32 kilometers and an altitude of 3,000 meters. This control zone also allowed military aircraft from the three Western powers to fly over East Berlin and border areas of East Germany. The altitude limit in the three corridors was not firmly established. Without protest, the Allies accepted the altitude limit of the Berlin zone for the corridors as well, which later proved a mistake. For with the arrival of the jet age, this low altitude proved uneconomical for jet flight. The Soviet Union would not be moved on the issue of the 3,000 meter ceiling, and rejected every Allied request to change it.

Despite all the other disagreements — the Soviets had withdrawn under protest from both the Allied Berlin Kommandatura as well as the Allied Governing Council (Kontrollrat), and they had closed their garrison headquarters (Stadtkommandatur) in East Berlin—the Soviets performed their duty in the Berlin Air Safety Center in a former courtroom in Schöneberg's Kleistpark correctly until the very last day. Every single flight had to be reported to and approved by the Center. The whole flight — both inbound and outbound — was electronically monitored. Although in the course of the years a whole series of incidents occurred, in general the air traffic was never seriously threatened. Provocative actions were more the rule.

On September 14, 1961, Soviet fighters buzzed two airliners belonging to the American airline Pan Am, with another Pan Am plane harassed two days later. On February 12, 1962, Soviet fighters conducted dangerous maneuvers near three American passenger planes. On the 9th of March, 1962, Soviet fighters launched chaff canisters in the air corridors, in order to disrupt the Western powers' radar and radio traffic. Each time the Western powers reacted with protests.

In addition, Soviet fighters would often swoop over West Berlin in steep dives, causing sonic booms to be heard. On July 6–7 the Soviet fighters' nose dives came to a veritable orgy. Apparently the Soviets' aim was to drive the Bundestag (Parliament), which was meeting on those two days in the Berlin Reichstag, out of Berlin, their rationale being that since West Berlin did not belong to West Germany, these meetings were illegal. The mass sorties were not without success: from then on, by request of the Allies, no further plenary sessions of the Bundestag took place in Berlin. Only committee meetings at which issues concerning Berlin were discussed were allowed.

One highly unusual case occurred on September 14th, 1961. Completely unexpectedly, two fighter-bombers of the Bundesluftwaffe (West German Air Force) appeared and landed at the civilian Tegel Airport. The answer to the puzzle: the pilots had taken part in a NATO manoeuvre in West Germany and had become lost at an altitude of eleven kilometers due to a severe thunderstorm. The French authorities handled the matter with the utmost discretion: both machines were completely disassembled and the pieces were transported to West German territory. The Soviets reacted quietly, most probably because it was embarrassing that their own air forces had failed to detect the two West German planes in time.

Air traffic to and from West Berlin was plagued by another development: the airports of West Berlin increasingly proved ideal destinations for refugees: on April 9th, 1978, two East German citizens landed in a sport plane at the British military airport Gatow. On the 24th of July, 1979, a sailplane coming from East Germany landed at Gatow also. On August 30th, 1978, an East German citizen forced the pilots of a Polish airliner en route from Danzig to Warsaw to change course for West Berlin. As he left the plane with his wife and child, six more East German citizens spontaneously joined him.

Polish air pirates also appeared with increasing frequency as refugees in West Berlin. At least fifteen times they arrived in aircraft belonging to the Polish airline LOT, which was soon nicknamed "L-ands O-ften in T-empelhof". All of the hijackers were sentenced by Western courts to up to four years imprisonment, although the sentences were suspended.

This Polish refugee movement reached its zenith on September 18, 1981. On that day twelve Poles — nine men and three women — took control of a Type AN-24 LOT airplane flying from Kattowitz to Warsaw and forced it to land at Tempelhof. In addition to the twelve hijackers, eight of the remaining 37 passengers also decided to request political asylum.

Quixotic Escape Attempts

The obstacles along the zone border became increasingly watertight, the alarm system ever more refined. In between stood the "Border Wall 75", solid and 3.6 meters tall. The time was over where there was any chance to storm the Wall boldly and climb over before the guards could mobilize. The number of refugees who were arrested while they were still in the border zone grew steadily, and a number of show trials for "Refugees from the Republic" had a chilling effect on the number of escape attempts. On the other hand, the number of ingenious escape attempts grew, where inventive methods were employed to fool the guards. One of the boldest of these attempts was described in the Wall Chronicles on July 28, 1965.

Heinz Holzapfel, a doctor of economics from Leipzig, often had official duties to perform in the "House of Ministers" on Wilhelmstraße. The building's southern wing directly abutted the zone border. The Leipziger had thought up a clever plan: on the far side of the south wing, on the West Berlin side of the Wall, his relatives waited under cover of darkness equipped with a steel cable six millimeters thick and 50 meters long. In addition a truck trailer had been pulled up to which the cable would be attached.

On that 28th of July, Holzapfel sneaked into a bathroom on the top floor of the "House of Ministers" with his wife Jutta and nine-year-old son Günter, hung a pre-made "Out of Order" sign on the door, and locked himself in with his family to await the close of business and darkness. At 10 p. m., the time that had been prearranged with his relatives, he threw a hammer wrapped in foam rubber far over the Wall. It was painted in bright colors, and tied to its handle was a one millimeter nylon line which Holzapfel held in his hand. His relatives found the hammer amidst the high weeds and attached the steel cable to the nylon line. Holzapfel hauled the contraption up with all his might. In this he had to be particularly careful, because only a few meters away on the roof of the "House of Ministers" was a guard post, in which a Soviet guard was stationed.

The now tightly-stretched wire cable, fastened to the flag pole on the roof, functioned as a cable car. The first passenger was the nine-year-old son, firmly strapped on with a chest and shoulder belt, and he soared over the precipice and over the Wall into the arms of his waiting relatives. The next trip was made by his wife Jutta, and last came the bold inventor — the escape of an entire family was a success. There was only one glitch: Holzapfel had hung a satchel filled with personal documents around his neck on a leather strap. The strap broke and the satchel landed with a loud thud in the courtyard of the "House of Ministers". Despite that, the sensational escape was not discovered until after daybreak.

Two East Berliners thought up a similar maneuver. In the direct vicinity of Checkpoint Charlie, they forced their way into the building housing the publisher of the newspaper "Neue Zeit" and cut through the window bars. Next they threw a 20 meter long cable attached to a small anchor out the window and over the Wall, where it took hold in the loose earth. Held aloft by the cable they glided down and landed safely in the district of Kreuzberg in the U. S. sector.

Many more nervy and outrageous escape attempts are recorded in the Wall Chronicles: in 1966 two laborers on board an 18-ton bulldozer tangoed through the Wall, which at that time was not yet unconquerable as the "Border Wall 75" would be. Their vehicle sported 38 bullet holes. Only one of the two refugees was slightly grazed on the head. In the spring of 1962, an olive-green Soviet-made "Pobyeda" station wagon with a Soviet major at the wheel passed through

Checkpoint Charlie, obviously unchallenged. The only problem: the major was no major, but a disguised East Berliner. He had assumed the identity of a Soviet officer. Utilizing a similar ruse, refugees disguised as American soldiers also made it through the Checkpoint. And in another case, three East Berlin medical students disguised as East German border guards reached the Steinstücken enclave.

Near the Friedrichstraße Bahnhof, where the intercity trains departed towards the first West Berlin station, Lehrter, the tracks ran for a few meters along the viaduct which fronted East Berlin houses. That fact was exploited by a group of twelve upper schoolers, who leaped one after the other on to the slowly moving train and thus reached the West three minutes later.

On January 20th, 1986, visitors to the Wall standing on an observation platform held their breath: in broad daylight 23-year-old telephone engineer Andreas Bratke suddenly raced across the white border strip which marked the border at Checkpoint Charlie — and thanks to the astonishment of the guards escaped uninjured. He had been employed in the testing of the electric security system, and had taken advantage of an unguarded moment to make a break for it.

Equally spectacular was the escapade in which the flagship of the East Berlin excursion fleet, the steamer "Friedrich Wolf", suddenly popped up in West Berlin waters: five crew members had overpowered the captain. Altogether fourteen refugees disembarked. A refugee sprang over the rail of the East German cruise ship "Völkerfreundschaft" as it sailed through the Bosporus. After making his way across Turkey, he safely reached the West. Another escape via waterways was accomplished by a cook and an electrician in September 1981. In the guise of blind passengers they sneaked onto an East German coal barge. As soon as the vessel entered West Berlin waters, they jumped overboard. Yet another successful maritime escape: hidden in the stinking waste water tank of an East German cargo barge, a married couple had set out along with their

son and daughter. Once the barge reached West Berlin territory, they simply climbed out.

Escape in a Balloon ...

Among the most adventurous escape attempts belongs a
flight in a hot air balloon from East German Thüringen to West
German Bavaria. Four adults and four children floated away
over all the barricades and guards during the clear night of
September 16, 1979, and landed safely after thirty minutes
aloft.

Peter Strelzyk, at the time 50 years of age, and his wife Doris
were the architects of the plan. They lived in the Thüringian
city of Pößneck and found the political situation there un-
bearable. Together with another married couple, they decided to take action. They crisscrossed East Germany in countless trips in order to accumulate scarce materials like taffeta,
nylon thread, and lining material. They needed approximately 1,200 square meters of material for their balloon. Peter
Strelzyk, who was an experienced electrical technician, improvised an ignition system out of four propane bottles that
would deliver the necessary hot air to the balloon.

Absolute secrecy was the first priority, and that alone was
difficult enough. Fear of informers was a constant compan-
ion. Nevertheless, the finished balloon was inflated to the
size of an eight story house. Strelzyk said after the flight:
"I still can't understand how the Stasi failed to discover our
preparations, which went on for weeks."

Safely landed in the Bavarian hamlet of Naila, their problems were by no means solved. On the contrary: the successful escape attempt became known not only to the Western
public but also to the East German secret police. Apparently,
they wanted to make an example of Peter Strelzyk. Anony-
mous hate mail arrived. There were threats of kidnapping.
What was more, a bomb attack was carried out on the Strel-

zyks' small electronics shop in Bad Kissingen. The Strelzyks were constantly "on the run": within a decade they had moved thirteen times—but the secret police inevitably picked up their trail. It wasn't until 1989, when the Wall had fallen, that all their fears were over. Shortly thereafter, the Strelzyks moved back to their Thüringian home.

... and Under the Earth

They clambered over the Wall, they slid down cables, they came by airplane or ship, and they escaped in homemade hot air balloons. These unusual escape attempts were joined by endeavors deep under the earth's surface. In the first years after the Wall was built, hundreds of people escaped in self-dug tunnels. Some of these tunnels were months in the digging. The excavations had to be carried out in the strictest secrecy, whereby the greatest problem was posed by the need for stealth in the disposal of the earth.

The first successful subterranean escape took place on January 24, 1962, in the Oranienburgian Schausee, where 28 East German citizens arrived safe and sound in the West. Another tunnel at the Oranienburgian Chausee was dug in the spring of 1962. The participants were mostly senior citizens, with an 81-year-old man leading the operation. Their tunnel was 32 meters long and in places 1.75 meters high. Through this excavation twelve people made it to freedom on May 5, 1962. During the month of June 1962 alone, a total of 25 East Germans from Britz, Hermsdorf, and Neukölln tunneled their way into the Western part of the city. Among the refugees was a four-month-old infant, who was towed through the tunnel in a tin basin by his father. Another 29 people, among them six children, escaped on September 18, 1962 through a 120-meter-long tunnel, which ended in the Schwedter Straße in the northern part of Berlin.

Not every undertaking was successful, however. The secret

View through the escape tunnel at Schwedter Straße, through which 29 refugees reached freedom in September 1962.

police succeeded in infiltrating informants among the groups in West Berlin which provided escape help. The members of these groups were in the beginning mostly idealists ready for anything, but they were inexperienced in guarding against sabotage and intelligence operations. Thus it was that in an escape tunnel originating in Neukölln's Elsenstraße a 21-year-old West Berlin escape advisor was shot to death by East German border guards. In other escape tunnels it came to wild shootouts, whereby two members of the border guards' own ranks lost their lives. They were praised as "Martyrs" by East German propaganda, although it was never completely ascertained whether they might not have been killed by their own comrades' hail of bullets. The well-known bicycle racer Harry Seidel would fall victim to a traitor also. He was a participant in the construction of a tunnel leading from Düppel in the region of Zehlendorf in the U. S. sector to the East. Seidel, who had already been involved in the construction of four previous tunnels, was arrested and sentenced to life in prison at a show trial 44 days later for "crimes against the peace." After four years, the West German government bought him free. In another show trial in August 1962, two East and three West Berliners were likewise sentenced to long jail terms. The court handed down two life sentences, one of 21 years, and in two cases terms of six and eight years.

Possibly the most spectacular tunnel project was based in the Bernauer Straße, which bordered the French Sector. From the cellar of an abandoned bakery, 38 West Berliners, including ten students, worked in shifts for six months on a tunnel which ended in an East Berlin coal yard. It was 145 meters long, but only 70 centimeters high, so that one had to crawl through it. During the nights of October 3–5, 1964, 57 refugees escaped this way to the West. It could well have been more, but on the third day of the undertaking the tunnel was discovered. A short time later it was blown up by the East German border guards. Among the students who were involved in the construction of the tunnel was one young man whose participation would make him famous: Reinhard Furrer became an astronaut, and was the first West German to be launched into space, on board Spacelab Flight D 1 in November, 1985. On September 9th, 1995, his life was destined to end tragically — he crashed his Messerschmitt Me-108 "Typhoon" on the grounds of Berlin's Johannistal flight research institute while on a precision flying exercise.

The tunnel builders of the "first generation" were certain to hear the cheers of the West Berliners. They financed most of their considerable expenses through private gifts. However, as over the course of time the readiness to give began to wane, the process of aiding refugees through tunnels became commercialized. Prices ranged up to several thousand D-marks per refugee. Towards the end, the secret police were increasingly successful at placing informants among the refugee assistance organizations, quickly destroying them. As a result, the tunnel businesses in West Berlin fell into political disfavor. They would ultimately die out as a result of the ever-increasing risk of discovery.

Building Legends on Dead Border Guards

In 1990 the former state and party leader Erich Honecker declared that he was ready to give a no-holds-barred interview, which would be conducted by the journalists Reinhold Andert and Wolfgang Herzberg. The interview later appeared as a book ("The Fall", Aufbau-Verlag). Honecker, who had been deposed in 1989, was asked, "Don't you regret that perhaps two hundred people were killed on the Wall?" Honecker responded: "I am sorry for our 25 comrades, who were treacherously murdered on the border."

That number — 25 dead border guards — would stand up to Western scrutiny after the collapse. The deaths of these men, however, was obscured in a haze of Communist legend building. Until the end of the East German regime, they were honored as "Heroes of the Socialist Fatherland". Schools and units of the National People's Army were named after them. Most of them were posthumously decorated with the "Combat Order of Service to the People and the Fatherland".

The investigation by the West Berlin group "Arbeitsgemeinschaft 13. August" of a list published in East Germany of victims of "armed attacks and imperialist provocations" brought to light a completely different set of facts: eleven of these border guards had been shot not by "Imperialists", but by their own comrades who were fleeing West. A border guard was shot by a deserting Soviet soldier. Civilian refugees had shot back at pursuing border guards in three cases. In two cases, soldiers lost their lives in escape tunnels, where it is certainly possible that they were struck down by bullets from their own ranks. In only two cases were the fatal shots fired by the weapons of American soldiers, and only once by those of the West Berlin police. In those cases it was a matter of protecting refugees who had already reached West German territory from the fire of the Eastern border guards. The rest of the incidents could not be clarified.

The death of East German border guard lance-corporal Peter Göring occurred on May 23, 1962 in the following manner: the 14 year-old upper-schooler Wilfried Thews had come to Berlin from the Thüringian city of Erfurt in order to escape over the Wall at the Spandauer Schiffahrtskanal. He had already scaled the Wall in the vicinity of the Invaliden-Friedhof (Veterans' cemetery) and jumped into the canal when he was discovered by a large patrol, which opened fire. Hit repeatedly and severely wounded, he nevertheless reached the western bank. He sought refuge in a niche in the stone embankment while West Berlin police tried to give the wounded man cover. Although the East Berlin border sentries had ceased their fire, Lance-Corporal Göring continued to fire on alone. When the West German police returned fire to protect the refugee, Göring was mortally wounded.

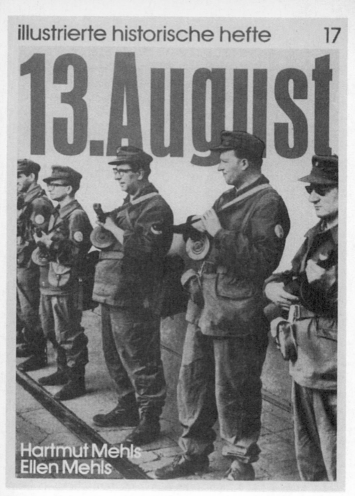

Because GDR politicians could not keep the Wall's construction secret, they sought to justify and glorify it. The propaganda text "August
13th" of 1979 is written in that language.

Ihr Tod ist uns
Verpflichtung

Uffz. Reinhold Huhn
Uffz. Helmut Just · Uffz. Jürgen Schmidchen
Uffz. Peter Göring
Uffz. Egon Schultz · Uffz. Siegfried Widera
Uffz. Rolf Henniger

Memorial to border guards who lost their lives in the line of duty. The picture shows the now-demolished monument on Schützenstraße, then called Reinhold-Huhn-Straße, directly behind the Verlagshaus Axel Springer.

The border guard Reinhold Kuhn was killed on June 18, 1962, as he tried to search a family of four which was on the verge of escaping to the West through a tunnel they had excavated. The father of the family thereupon drew a pistol and killed the border guard. The 21-year-old border sentry Egon

Schultz was killed when refugees heading west crawled on their hands and knees along Berlin's longest escape tunnel, on Bernauer Straße. In the gloom of the tunnel, a firefight broke out between the border guards and the refugees — it remained an open question whether the soldier was killed by the weapon of a refugee or one of his own comrades.

Over 2,000 Deserters

At first the East German government deployed only those who had enlisted in the army on guard duty in the rural areas along the fortified frontier. Starting in 1962, draftees were also utilized in order to guarantee the necessary full-time force of 50,000 men. This, however, increased the risk of desertions for the regime. Consequently, the border guards came under increased supervision. In principle they were allowed out on patrol only in twos or threes. In addition, they were to be observed by their officers stationed in nearby watch towers. A special unit of the state security organs, designated "Administration 2000", was utilized also in supervising the border guards. Their job was to ferret out escape plans among the soldiers with the help of spies, some of whom were volunteers and others who had volunteered under pressure.

Within the first six weeks after the construction of the Wall, the border guard had suffered 85 cases of desertion. In that context a West Berlin photojournalist snapped a once-in-a-lifetime shot: it caught the 19-year-old junior officer Conrad Schumann throwing away his rifle as he leaped over the still-provisional barricades in full uniform. The photo was published all over the world. One of the most spectacular escapes occurred at the Berlin Wall in April, 1963: a group of NVA soldiers crashed through the the barricades in an armored personnel carrier and a truck and escaped to West Berlin uninjured.

In November, 1965, Honecker learned of a report in the West

Probably the world's most famous photo of a GDR-refugee: 19-year-old junior officer Conrad Schumann leaped over the barbed wire at Bernauer Straße on August 15, 1962.

Berlin newspaper "Die Zeit", which said that there had been 122 cases of desertion in the third quarter of that year, which represented a significant increase over the comparable figure of 94 deserters in the third quarter of 1964. This story caused Honecker to gather his NVA commanders in order to question them about the report's accuracy. The generals had to quietly admit that the actual figures were even higher: 143 cases of desertion in the third quarter of 1965, compared to 107 cases in the corresponding period of the previous year. The total number of deserters is estimated to be at least 2,000, with some estimates as high as 2,700.

Despite the many tragedies along the Wall and the intra-German border, there were many examples of humanity as well. The high number of desertions alone showed that many soldiers could ease their consciences only by fleeing to the West. Rainer Hildebrandt, the director of the Mauer Museum on Berlin's Friedrichstraße, has a story to tell: the whole time there were border guards who sent secret signals of protest to Western observers. While some of them had their eyes glued to their binoculars, the others signalled surreptitiously with their little fingers. Some covertly drew the sign of the cross over their Kalashnikovs. Sometimes protest notes wrapped around rocks were thrown over the Wall.

The Protests Never Stopped

Even over the course of 28 years an accomodation with the Wall could never be coerced. Again and again it came to national and international protests. It was not just West Berliners whose protests had to be restrained by their own police forces in order to avoid dangerous confrontations, but also a great many foreigners who protested the construction of the Wall and the tragedies that resulted therefrom. A few stories out of the many are presented here.

In 1961 a Lebanese salesman repeatedly tried to force his way into East German territory, in order to plant a large cross bearing the inscrption "Freedom" in English and Arabic. In 1964 the Gandhi follower Carl-Wolfgang Holzapfel attempted to enter the Soviet sector with a placard demanding the release of the bicycle racer Harry Seidel, who had been sentenced to life in prison for aiding and abetting escape attempts. Twice he was turned back by the border guards, and on the third attempt he was arrested and sentenced to eight years in prison. Thirteen months later his freedom was purchased by the West German government. The "Society for German-Italian Friendship" also stepped into the limelight with repeated protests in Berlin as well as in Italy. On September 1, 1983, the Western peace movement, whose members possessed Western passports and so were able to enter East Berlin freely, sought to build a human daisy chain along Unter den Linden between the U.S. embassy building and the nearby

Soviet embassy. The demonstators were scattered by the police within the first few minutes, and five of them were arrested. Also, on August 9, 1986, about 150 people sought to push their way into the Soviet sector at Checkpoint Charlie to mount a protest. That attempt resulted in violent clashes with the border guards.

Probably the most farcical protest against the Wall, one which created an enormous stir, was choreographed by a then-68-year-old cabinetmaker from the American city of Seattle named John Runnings. In 1968 he traveled to Berlin, climbed on top of the Wall and, brooking no interference from either West Berlin policemen or Western military officers, proceeded to balance his way along the top of the Wall for 500 meters. East German border guards finally got a ladder and forced him off onto the East German side. Apparently the GDR was afraid of international repercussions, because Runnings was promptly sent back to West Berlin unmolested.

There were always those who could not accept the inhuman division. Here young demonstrators took to the streets at Checkpoint Charlie on the 25th anniversary of the Wall's construction.

Perhaps the most original protest was mounted by the American John Runnings, who repeatedly climbed the Wall in 1986 and 1987 with a sledgehammer.

The American, however, did not have the slightest intention of quitting. In West Berlin he announced: "I will show you, how one can exercise political influence on the Wall. Military confrontations must be answered with political challenges."

A second stroll atop the Wall followed quickly. This time, Runnings symbolically knocked off small pieces of the Wall's concrete with a hammer. Once again, he was forced down by the border guards, and one day later again set free. On his third stroll on the Wall, he was accompanied by a 19-year-old German. While the American was again freed after 53 hours of confinement, the German remained in jail. Runnings promptly appeared at Checkpoint Charlie, stepped onto East German territory, and refused to leave. His efforts actually succeeded in freeing the German. At that point, the American authorities decided to send him back to the United States by plane from the airport at Frankfurt am Main. Upon his arrival there, he immediately set out on a new journey to Berlin. Once in the divided city, he again climbed the Wall. This time the East German authorities reacted differently: Runnings remained in jail for a period of two months. Then the East Germans brought him to Prague, where he was put on a Soviet Aeroflot plane bound for New York.

However, this man, who had previously protested against the Vietnam war and the nuclear arms race, was not done yet. He appeared yet again in Berlin, and constructed a gigantic wooden ram. It was to be wielded against the Wall by fourteen brawny men, an undertaking which, considering the sturdy construction of the "modern" Wall, did not stand a chance of success. In any event, the West Berlin police were faster. Before the enterprise could proceed further, they confiscated the contraption on the orders of the U. S. occupation forces. It can still be seen today in the museum at Checkpoint Charlie.

Statesmen From All Over The World On The Wall

Politicians and statesmen from all over the world visited the Wall. For guests from Western countries, part of the protocol while visiting West Germany was a detour to Berlin to see the Wall. Official guests of the East German government signed their names in a visitors' book at the Brandenburger Tor, climbed the observation towers facing West Germany, or took in the expanse of the Wall from one of the balconies of the Reichstag building. Khrushchev, who had given the construction of the Wall his personal consent, stood on the Wall for the first time on January 17, 1963. He chose Checkpoint Charlie as the site for his visit. Photos taken from the Western side show him smiling and looking challengingly toward the West. Only a few months earlier, Khrushchev had had to swal-

January 17, 1963: GDR-Premier Walter Ulbricht (with beard) showed the Berlin Wall to USSR State and Party leader Nikita Khrushchev (with upraised hand).

low a defeat which would contribute heavily to his downfall in 1964: in the Cuban crisis — the high- and turning-point of the Cold War — the United States had successfully intervened by means of a sea blockade in the stationing of Soviet missiles on Cuban soil.

His opponent John F. Kennedy saw the Wall five months later, on June 26, 1963. His first stop was the Brandenburg Tor. The Communists, however, were prepared: The arch was so thickly draped with red cloth that the American President could not see the Unter den Linden, nor could the East Germans see the American President. Kennedy also paid a complimentary visit to Checkpoint Charlie. Together with Chancellor Konrad Adenauer and Berlin's incumbent Mayor Willy Brandt, he climbed the observation platform on the Wall. Kennedy's visit to Berlin became a unique triumphal procession. Hundreds of thousands of people swarmed into the

U. S. President John F. Kennedy accompanied by Chancellor Konrad Adenauer and Mayor Willy Brandt. Visibly moved, he listened to explanations of events at Checkpoint Charlie.

streets and cheered. Hundreds of thousands more crowded onto the square in front of the Schöneberger Rathaus, where in his speech Kennedy delivered the often-quoted line, "Ich bin ein Berliner."

U. S. President Ronald Reagan delivered his historic speech in front of the Brandenburger Tor on June 12, 1987.

On April 16, 1986 a delegation of the Communist Party of the Soviet Union in East Berlin attended the SED's 11th Party Convention. One of the guests is Mikhail Gorbachov.

For the West German population, still in a state of psychological shock due to the bisection of their city, the day of Kennedy's visit was like casting off a burden. The visit stabilized a new-found self-confidence and brought the Berliners still closer together with the strongest of their Protecting Powers.

After John F. Kennedy, the U. S. Presidents Richard Nixon, Jimmy Carter, and George Bush also came. President Ronald Reagan's visit, with his speech in front of the Brandenburger Tor, turned into an grandiose political demonstration. At the end of his speech before the Brandenburger Tor, the President called out to the Soviet leader Mikhail Gorbachev in Moscow: "General Secretary Gorbachev, if you are striving toward peace, if you wish for prosperity for the Soviet Union and Eastern Europe, if you want liberalization, then come here to this Gate. Mister Gorbachev, open this Gate! Mister Gorbachev, tear down this Wall!"

Travel Passes — The Great Christmas Joy

Until Christmas of 1963, West German citizens had the "privilege" of visiting East Berlin; up to that point the West Berliners had been shut out. Shortly after the construction of the Wall the East German government had offered to establish branch offices of the state travel agencies on West Berlin territory, in which East Berlin personnel would be used to dispense entry visas. However, the three Western allies declined the offer: to them the intentions of the East Germans seemed all too transparent, namely surreptitiously acquiring sovereign rights in West Berlin and thus undermining the city's Four-Power-Status.

It was not until Christmas of 1963 that long negotiations between the West Berlin Senate Advisor Horst Korber and the East German Secretary of State Erich Wendt finally led to an agreement which allowed family visits in East Berlin from

A newlywed couple stood in front of the barricaded door of the senior citizens home on Bernauer Straße in September 1961. Their bewildered relatives could speak to the young couple only from third-floor windows. The wounds were still fresh when two years later the first exit visas were issued.

Exit-visa Agreement, Christmas 1963: Thousands of people waited for the coveted papers in the freezing cold for hours in front of the distribution outlet on Charlottenberg's Schillerstraße.

Success! Meta Leusmann could now visit her relatives in East Berlin.

The customs barracks at the border crosspoint at the Friedrichstraße Bahnhof.

December 19 until January 5, 1964. The city experienced some touching "until we meet again" scenes during those days. Altogether a total of 1,242,800 one-day-passes were issued from the entry visa outlets, which had been provisionally set up in school buildings. The personnel were provided by the Eastern post office administration. For each of these visits, which were limited to one day, ten D-marks had to be changed into East German currency (Ostmarks) in a one-to-one ratio; unspent money could not be changed back. Entry into East Berlin had to occur between the hours of 6 a. m. and 8 p. m., and the return had to be made no later than midnight.

Thereafter, there were six more entry-visa "windows", the last one from May 23 to June 5, 1966. Thereafter a multi-year hiatus set in, as the two sides could not come to terms. During this period, however, under the terms of the pass agreement of 1964, there remained one "Entry Visa Outlet for Urgent Family Affairs". Entry visas were dispensed for the following

First reunion after two years of separation.

situations: births, divorces, life-threatening illnesses, and the deaths of parents, children, siblings, grandparents or uncles/aunts. Only in 1972, after negotiations between the West Berlin Senate and the East German government, were new visiting procedures established which were much more leniently framed and took as their starting point the 1971 "Agreement

With the signing of the Visa Agreement of 1972 it was possible for greater numbers of people to visit the other part of Germany. Enormous customs facilities had to be built, like this one at the Drewitz checkpoint near Potsdam.

on Easements and Improvements to the Travel- and Visitor Traffic". The agreement came into effect on June 3, 1972, and also covered those foreigners who had a permanent residence in West Berlin. It allowed 30 visiting days per year. In 1984, the number of yearly visiting days was raised to 45. Applications had to be submitted to one of five West Berlin "Offices for Visiting and Travel Affairs". For reasons of status the Allies insisted that while the applications could be collected by East Berlin personnel, they could only be processed in East Berlin. The West Berlin police provided security in the entry visa outlets, thus ensuring that the sovereign rights would remain in West Berlin hands.

A further liberalization occurred after new negotiations in 1987: there were now multiple-entry passes, which were valid for six months. In 1988 multiple-entry passes were introduced that allowed ten visits. By July 1, 1982, the curfew for day visits had been extended until 2 a. m. In March 1988 two-day passes were inaugurated, and in August 1989 a new regulation allowed visits to the East German regions of Frankfurt/ Oder and Potsdam. During the years 1972 to 1989 the yearly numbers of West Berlin visitors hovered between 2,078,000 and 2,379,000. For each day trip every visitor over the age of 16 had to pay five D-marks, and 15 D-marks for multiple-day passes.

How Prisoners Were Ransomed

On September 23, 1963, a top-secret event took place in the GDR. To their complete surprise, three political prisoners who had been behind bars for years were escorted out of their cells, handed their luggage, and turned over to an East Berlin lawyer. He brought them to West Berlin in his car, and there delivered them to a West Berlin lawyer — the three were free.

This surprising release was preceded by secret contacts between middlemen from the East and West. The Western side was sent a signal that the GDR was prepared to a great extent to release political prisoners, if the Western side was prepared to make financial remuneration for them. These secret meetings at unofficial levels came to the attention of the publisher Axel Springer. In a conversation with the newly-appointed Minister for All-German Affairs, Rainer Barzel (CDU), Springer volunteered to establish such a ransom system for political prisoners. Barzel succeeded in selling the plan to the government.

The exchanges came to pass. For quite a while the releases were kept quiet. Initially the Western side paid cash, in West German currency, and later payment was made by deliveries of raw materials. The per-head price for each prisoner released was initially 40,000 D-marks. The GDR was able to raise the price continually, so that by the end it had risen to almost 100,000 D-marks. The Diaconic Work of the Protestant Church emerged as a negotiating partner of the the West German government. It gathered information on materials in which the GDR was particularly interested. The West German government secretly hoped to help the East German population with their serious problems in the area of foodstuffs. This hope, however, did not materialize. The GDR constantly demanded deliveries of crude oil, copper, silver, and industrial diamonds, which for the most part they sold for cash on the international raw materials markets. The organizational responsibility for carrying out the ransoming of prisoners was borne on the Eastern side by the lawyer Wolfgang Vogel and on the Western side by his colleague Jürgen Stange.

More than once it was supposed by the Western side that after this agreement the East German government was prepared to be very "generous" regarding prison sentences for political offenses. No such tendency could ever be discerned. The Western side was taken in on a number of occasions: criminal prisoners were substituted for political prisoners. In the interests of the bigger picture, the West German government let these cases drop.

The longtime Secretary of State Ludwig A. Rehlinger was responsible on behalf of the West German government for the ransomings. In his book "Ransom — The East German Trade in the Politically Prosecuted, 1963–1989", Rehlinger balanced the books as follows: as a result of ransoms, 33,755 prisoners were released before their sentences were up. Over 2,000 children, mostly left behind by refugees for security reasons, were reunited with their families. Lastly, over 250,000 families were reunited. The Western side furnished cash and deliveries of raw materials in the amount of over 3.5 billion D-marks. In addition to these officially sanctioned ransoms, there was an unofficial kind as well. Thus the case of a female doctor came to light, who was allowed to travel to West Germany after a payment of 200,000 D-marks had been made.

After the collapse of the Wall, examination of East German files revealed what the regime had done with the money earned in this way: continuous supplies of Western goods for the VIP-enclave of Wandlitz, expenditures for communist sister parties in the West, financing the 30th anniversary of the founding of the GDR, solidarity outlays for Nicaragua, furnishment of 160 Citroën limousines for prominent figures in the Party and government, and deposits in bank accounts abroad.

Even Explosives Were Smuggled

People crossed over the Wall in many ways — they were smuggled out of East Berlin in diplomatic cars as were icons, caviar, and, ultimately, explosives. The remarkable thing about this particular type of contraband was that it reached West Berlin with the knowledge and approval of the Stasi. On August 25, 1983, a powerful bomb exploded in the French culture center "Maison de France" on Kurfürstendamm. One person was killed and 23 injured, some of them severely. The circle of suspects came to include the Armenian terrorist group "Asala". The Western investigators would not get the whole story until after the collapse of the Wall, when it became possible to examine secret files. They revealed that the East German secret police had complete knowledge of the preparations and timing of the attack. They knew about not only the transport of the 24 kilos of explosives through Checkpoint Charlie, but also the identities of the terrorists, who carried Yemenite and Syrian diplomatic passports. After carrying out the attack the terrorists were permitted to travel untouched into East Berlin and from there continue on to Budapest, Damascus, and Belgrade.

After the Wall fell, similar information was uncovered in the files of the East German secret police in the case of the April 5, 1986 bombing of the discoteque "La Belle" in the

American sector, which was frequented by U.S. soldiers. That attack resulted in three dead and 230 wounded, many of them seriously. The trail quickly led to Libya. The "smoking gun", however, was not found until after the Wall fell: the Stasi had been fully informed from the beginning about the planned attack, according to File II/15 from the Chief Directorate of the Stasi, dated January 29, 1987. The secret police had at the time initiated "Operation Vorgang" ("OV"), and Minister Erich Mielke had ordered the bombers to be kept under constant surveillance, but that no actions were to be taken against any of their activities aimed at West Berlin. The contents of these documents leaves no doubt that the Stasi worked hand-in-hand with Arab terrorists.

The Stasi also provided assistance to German terrorists of the Baader-Meinhof Gang in the cases of the assassins Werner Lotze, Silke Maier-Witt, Suzanne Albricht, and Sigrid Sternebeck. They found refuge from the West German dragnet in East Germany, where they were provided with new identities. It was only after the collapse of the Wall that they were discovered and could finally be brought to justice.

The Four-Power-Agreement of 1972

In accord with the axiom "Trust in God, but tie up your horse", the policies of aggression and de-escalation often ran parallel in East Germany. The goal of de-escalation policy was to achieve the appearance of a responsible state which respected the principles of human rights in the interests of gaining international recognition. In the years following the collapse of the Wall the political climate began to thaw. Granted, the Soviets had sought to undermine the Four-Power-Status in Berlin in that they had quit the joint adminstration (Kommandatura) and had pro forma dismissed the staff of the Soviet administration, but the Status still remained in force. Thus, for example, the four victorious powers worked together

How the Berliners rearranged their lives over the years in the shadow of the Wall is illustrated by this photo.

quite properly in the Spandau Prison for war criminals — every four weeks another power would assume the guard and supervisory duties. In the Air Safety Center in Schöneberg the cooperation also ran smoothly, despite some unfortunate incidents which occurred over the years and which were never satisfactorily explained. As in the past, the Western portion of the city stood under the protective umbrella of NATO, whose members were obligated to "consider any attack against Berlin ... as an attack on their own armed forces and themselves". In addition there was the presence of Western troops, which until the collapse of the Wall consisted of 12,300 men. For the time being the West German Army was forbidden to set foot into the city.

After years of Soviet propaganda claims that the Western powers no longer had the right to be present in Berlin, efforts at de-escalation finally led to an agreement on September 3, 1971, after 18 months of tough bargaining between the am-

The Schönenberg Boys' Choir on December 21, 1964 at the Ober-baumbrücke. Musical protest against the division of Berlin or PR-event in a gruesomely macabre setting?

bassadors of the four powers. It not only mandated a whole series of liberalizations for West Berliners, but also "cemented" the rights and responsibilities of the three Western powers. Their access rights to and their presence in West Berlin were safeguarded, as was the city's NATO protection. In addition, the Four-Power-Status of the city proper was not disturbed.

The Soviet Union agreed to keep civilian traffic on the roads as well as the rail- and waterways free from impediments, and even liberalize it. West Berlin residents were now allowed to travel to East Berlin and the GDR for "humanitarian, family, religious, cultural and commercial" reasons or simply as tourists. To be sure, there were conditions: visits to Berlin as well as the various regions of the GDR were limited to 30 days per year. Longer visits had to be requested in writing by friends or relatives from the East.

In addition, the mail, telegram, and telephone connections were improved. After being completely cut off for over 20 years, Berliners from both parts of the city could talk to each other on the telephone. The West Berlin enclaves of Steinstücken and Eiskeller finally acquired access roads, which were no longer subject to East German control.

The Four-Power-Agreement was signed into law by the four foreign ministers of the Soviet Union, the U. S. A., Britain and France. It remained in effect until the Wall fell. The Agreement corresponded with Chancellor Willy Brandt's long-time "Policy of Small Steps", which was based on "Change through Closer Relations" (Egon Bahr).

Western Journalists Now Allowed In Also

On December 21, 1972, the Basic Treaty was negotiated by the two German states, which would "govern the foundations of the relations between the Federal Republic of Germany and the German Democratic Republic". Under the terms of that treaty, the two West German public television stations, ARD and ZDF, were granted permission to establish news bureaus in East Berlin. The accreditations became effective on March 7, 1973. The West German print media was

Unique media were employed to keep the "other side" informed during the early years of separation. The loudspeakers of the "Barbwire Studio" were clearly audible in the East ...

... while the illuminated teleprompters on the GSW-Haus on Koch-straße and at Potsdamer Platz (shown here) blinked reports from the free press over Berlin's Mitte district.

allowed to establish affiliates. In return, East German press organs opened offices in Bonn. However, the Western journalists were from the beginning under more or less constant surveillance by the Stasi and under the strict supervision of the regime's press department. Fact-finding missions to the different regions of the GDR had to be reported in advance. In most cases the journalists were provided with official escorts. Moreover, every interview had to be approved by the press office. It goes without saying that the person to be interviewed would be "coached" beforehand.

After just the first two years the first confrontations occurred: on December 16, 1975 the reporter for the news magazine "Der Spiegel" was expelled from East Berlin. One year later, on December 22, 1976, the same fate befell the ARD reporter Lothar Loewe. He alleged in a report that the number of arrests for political offenses had risen and that emigration applications were increasingly being withdrawn under threats of repression. In addition, he reported that it was universal knowledge that the border guards had orders "to shoot people like rabbits". On January 10, 1978, the East Berlin offices of "Der Spiegel" were closed. Those involved were accused of "continued and malicious slander of the GDR". On May 14, 1979, the ZDF correspondent Peter von Loyen was kicked out, followed on January 12, 1983 by Dieter Bub, a reporter for the Hamburg illstrated weekly "Stern". He was accused of "false and defamatory reporting".

Western press media could no longer legally be offered in the GDR. The population could stay informed by means of the West German national broadcasters, however, and they made overwhelming use of them. Only the area around Dresden could not receive West German television. In East German slang this region was nicknamed the "valley of the clueless".

Artists and the Wall

In 1966, the famous painter Oskar Kokoschka was persuaded to paint a city portrait of Berlin, as he had already done in Lyons and Hamburg. At first he was skeptical of the whole idea: "I have no idea if I can paint Berlin. I have scarcely slept for weeks and I am quite concerned about the portrait. Perhaps I will leave after two days."

Kokoschka did not leave. A studio was set up for him on the 19th floor of the Axel-Springer-Verlags building overlooking the Wall. There over the course of several weeks the oil portrait was born. The painter titled his work "The 13th of August, 1966", because that was the day the GDR passed the fifth anniversary of the founding of its "anti-fascist defensive wall", and a ceremonial procession wound its way along the death strip.

Kokoschka would later write about the conception of his work: "When for the first time I looked down into the red sector of Berlin, I grew afraid. A deserted wasteland, like a lunar landscape, separated from swarming life by boundary fences, accordions of barbed wire, and high voltage fences strung acrosss the streets. A guard dog set on a man lunged against his chain. I have never painted a ghost city before. There must still be people there — perhaps hidden in the concrete barracks ... in unison a regiment marches by under red flags in celebration of the founding of the Wall on August 13, 1961. A sentry patrols along the Wall, machine gun at the ready. No, there are two of them. Each has to guard the other."

Many other painters from Germany and many other countries accepted the challenge presented by the Wall. In the "Haus am Checkpoint Charlie" one can see a comprehensive permanent exhibit, which takes as its theme the collective separation of Berlin and Germany and its inhuman consequences. The many artists represented include Gisela Breitling, Traudbert Erbe, Jihannes Grützke, Hanna Höch, Matthias Koeppel, Jiri Kolar, Nikolai Makarov, Lydia Masterkova, Curt Mühlenhaupt, Lew Nussberg, Horst Strempel, Wolf Vostell, and Joe Zucker.

This does not say enough about the relationship which well-known German and foreign artists had with the Wall: in connection with the "modernization" of the "fourth Generation Wall", segments were manufactured that could seamlessly be joined together, a situation that had unexpected consequences for the builders: artists from many lands, both professionals and amateurs, discovered that the Wall now made a perfect canvas. Some of the results were serious, but others were humorous or risqué. In addition there were hundreds of inscriptions by visitors from all over the world. "Learn through suffering" one Londoner warned. An unknown artist came up with the consolation that "Nothing is forever". "Solidarity" was emblazoned repeatedly, and so was "Freiheit, Liberté, Liberty". "This here is the Wall, dear citizens" someone wrote rather condescendingly to the West Germans in the "Guest Book". One segment bore the inscription "This times 163,000 equals the Wall". "Erich, get out the key" was

Oskar Kokoschka with Axel Springer in the "Studio". The painting "Berlin—August 13, 1966" shows the view from the Springer building over the war-ravaged center of the city.

directed at the SED leader, in vain of course, as he was still claiming during his last year in power that the Wall could last for perhaps another hundred years if the "reasons for its construction" were not resolved. Another joker wrote, "Last one out turn off the lights", in reference to the unceasing flow of refugees in spite of the Wall and the ever-increasing numbers of emigration applications.

In 1984 Rainier Hildebrandt, who was not only the director of the Mauer-Museum but also the chairman of the "Arbeitsgemeinschaft 13. August", announced an international artists' competition entitled "Overcoming the Wall Through Its Paintings". Among the first artists to heed the call was the exiled Russian painter Lew Nussberg, who had settled in Berlin. Richard Hambleton created a 30-meter-long frieze, Christophe Bouchets an antediluvian animal park 400 meters

Newly pre-fabricated Wall segments lay on the other side of the border in Wedding ready for installation.

Graffiti on the Wall along Stresemannstraße in Kreuzberg. In the — formerly Eastern — background is the former Prussian parliament building, currently the House of Representatives of the reunited German capital.

long. Jonathan Borowsky and many others, principally from the U. S. A. and France, took part.

One particular attraction was the 1.3-kilometer "East Side Gallery" on East Berlin's Mühlenstraße. One picture became especially well-known: it shows Erich Honecker planting a kiss on the cheek of the then-Soviet leader Leonid Brezhnev. With the passage of time the "East Side Gallery" began to suffer from the ravages of weather. In 1996, 15 of the artists involved came to Berlin to restore their works.

Berlin: Background for Spy Novels

"The American handed Leamas another cup of coffee and said, 'Why don't you go back to sleep? We can ring you if he shows up.' Leamas said nothing, just stared out through the window of the checkpoint, along the empty street."

Thus begins the espionage novel "The Spy Who Came In From The Cold" (Rowohlt), by the Englishman John Le Carré. Berlin, playground for countless agents from countries all over the world, featuring the Wall with its undiscovered secrets, became the perfect backdrop for spy novels. Le Carré's story takes place in the divided city, at Checkpoint Charlie: Leamas, a British Secret Service agent, has orders from London headquarters to topple the chief agent of the opposition's secret service in East Berlin. It is an exciting story, written by a man capable of great insight, who was himself at one time involved in military intelligence — the thriller became a worldwide success, and was made into a movie starring Richard Burton.

Yet another British espionage novelist, Len Deighton, moved to Berlin. He also chose Checkpoint Charlie as the setting for his novel "Brahms Four" (Ullstein): two British agents spend night after night peering over the barricades toward East Berlin, waiting in vain for the master informant "Brahms Four", who had supplied London headquarters for many years with vital economic information. John Le Carré now faced real competition: British and American newspapers named Deighton as the "Number One" author of spy novels.

The successful American author Norman Mailer described

The Glienicker Brücke between Berlin and Potsdam had special significance for authors of espionage novels and also as the scene of actual agent exchanges.

Berlin in his book "Harlot's Ghost" as a "circus of espionage and counterespionage". A literary exaggeration, but it contained a kernel of truth: because after the construction of the Wall, East and West were increasingly involved in efforts to seek out the opposition's secrets. There were allegedly eight diplomatic attachés in the American Consulate in West Berlin who in reality were involved in undercover espionage for the GDR. The three military missions of the Western powers, which had been active on East German territory since 1946, had similar interests. Truth or exaggeration — the British Major Nigel Wylde claimed after the collapse of the Wall that the Western powers had been "95 % informed about the Red Army stationed in East Germany". The KGB alone occupied ten buildings in East Berlin. In addition, 74 rooms in the Stasi's headquarters building were placed at their disposal. While underway in the GDR, Western investigators were almost al-

On February 11, 1986, Soviet civil-rights activist Anatoly Shcharansky (in fur hat) was exchanged in the presence of U. S. Ambassador Richard Burt (at car door).

ways shadowed by Russian or East German escorts. Their assignment was to keep the unwelcome "guests" away from certain objectives. Occasionally, bloody disagreements erupted.

The Americans had constructed a radar dish that could be seen for miles on Berlin's Teufelberg to supervise the airways. The observation radius reached as far as the city of Minsk, capital of Byelorus.

From time to time "law and order" would be brought to the espionage business, in that the two sides would exchange their agents. The favorite spot for the exchanges was the Glienicker Brücke between Zehlendorf and Potsdam. It was here on February 10, 1962 that Gary Powers, the American pilot who had been shot down over Soviet Union during a reconaissance flight, was traded for Rudolf Abel, the master Soviet spy who had operated in the U. S. A. In June 1985 the Eastern side released 23 people who had been accused of espionage in exchange for the Bulgarian agent Penyu Kostadinov.

One man in particular achieved distinction in recruiting agents: as the director of the "First Espionage Directorate" of the Stasi, Markus Wolf achieved spectacular results. He succeeded in establishing a network that penetrated West Germany's uppermost echelons. After the collapse of the Wall, most of the GDR's espionage files were destroyed. However, there wasn't time to destroy them all. Investigative committees are still occupied today in efforts to reconstruct the surviving fragments.

"Day X" in the Drawer

Despite the Four-Power-Agreement and the Basic Treaty, with all their liberalizations for the West Berliners, and despite the politics of détente, the Eastern side always remained prepared for "Day X", the occupation of West Berlin. The details were spelled out in a document discovered after the collapse entitled "Detailed Orders of Berlin Sector Command". It was

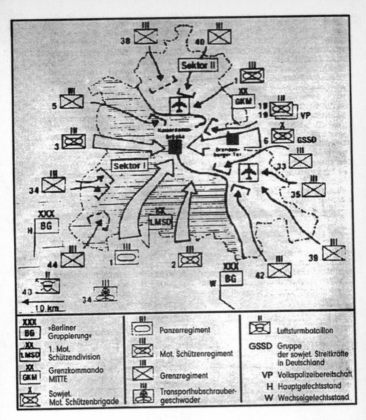

Sketch of the invasion plan, which was still being rehearsed in August 1985. Meanwhile, some Western politicians praised the peace loving nature of the East German regime.

signed on August 5, 1985 by Generalleutnant Schwanitz, the commander of the Berlin Sector and Mielke's personal representative. The document indicated that immediately after an occupation of West Berlin, thirteen secret police headquarters were to be established, which were to operate in close connection with Soviet army headquarters and the NVA.

Heroic deeds at the conquest of West Berlin were to be rewarded with the *Blücher Medal*. The medals were stored in great numbers in East Berlin vaults, ready to be handed out.

The better to discern the outlines of fleeing refugees, the "friendly" side of the Wall was regularly whitewashed. Perhaps that is why so many houses in East Berlin were gray.

In addition, West Berlin would find itself divided into two sections precisely at the moment the two onrushing columns of NVA troops, attacking from East and West, met at the Kaiserdammbrücke in Charlottenburg. The two airports, Tempelhof and Tegel, were to be stormed by air. Specific orders of engagement had been drawn up for a number of divisions, regiments, and specialized units. The Western allies' troop strength was estimated at 12,000 men, plus 6,000 West Berlin auxiliary police. Their own troop strength was put at 32,000.

At a military training base some 30 kilometers from the checkpoint at Dreilinden, comprehensive technical preparations were made for an invasion of West Berlin: a miniature model city complete with houses, streetcars, fake subway entrances, industrial areas and river banks served as a training ground for street and house-to-house fighting.

As early as May 1978 the 15th Reconnaiscence Department of the Stasi had prepared a list of 170 "vital strongpoints" in

The entire extent of the death strip was brilliantly illuminated every night. For 28 years.

West Berlin. They were incorporated into the Schwanitz files. On the day of the invasion of West Berlin, the Schöneberger Rathaus, Radio Free Berlin, the Springer Publishers building, and police headquarters were to be occupied first, along with the headquarters of political parties, long distance telephone offices, food wholesalers and other primary objectives. There were also plans to establish camps, which the Schwanitz plan describes as locations for the "Safekeeping of Hostile Forces". Among those to be arrested immediately were leading figures of the Berlin Senate, agents of the intelligence organizations, key figures from the business, science, and technology sectors, and well-known anti-Communist journalists.

All financial assets in the banks and warehouses were to be secured, and an occupation currency, christened "military money" in the plans, was to take the place of the D-mark. Even a new medal had been planned. It would be presented to those officers and men who had distinguished themselves during the occupation of West Berlin. The "Blücher Medal of Bravery" was established four months before the collapse of the Wall. 8,000 of the medals were stored in the "medal storage cellar" of the GDR Defense Ministry in Strausberg near Berlin.

The Stasi planned to field a force of 604 agents from their headquarters, of whom 343 were military officers. Pinpointing "hostile forces" was the job of the "unofficial agents" (known as IMs, for Inoffiziellen Mitarbeiter) and "secret agents" (GMs, for Geheimen Mitarbeiter), who had been smuggled into West Berlin or recruited there.

The Last Victims at the Wall

Former senior operatives of the East German intelligence organizations admitted after the collapse of the Wall that in the late Seventies and early Eighties, that is, during the period of détente, a time when the GDR was redoubling its efforts to achieve official recognition from the international community, every fatality at the Wall was a propaganda nightmare. According to these sources, they generated considerable internal debate. The ground rules remained firm, however: prevention of escape retained priority over all other considerations. The result was more refugee tragedies in the Eighties: on December 1, 1984, 20-year-old Michael Schmidt lay dead in no-man's-land. His father, alarmed by the fact that there was no sign of his son, initiated inquiries but was stonewalled by the East German authorities for four days with the explanation that nothing was known of any fatal accidents at the Wall. Reports to the contrary that appeared in the West Berlin press were to be regarded as "provocations". On November 24, 1986, 25-year-old Michael Bittner was shot dead. In addition, in 1989, the year the Wall fell, another refugee, the 20-year-old Chris Gueffroy, was killed on February 5. His case was described as follows in the "Confidential File No.

One of countless cases: in September 1971, an escape attempt at Lindenstraße between Kreuzberg and Mitte was stopped by well-aimed gunfire.

G/739022": "Arrest of Gueffroy, Chris, DOB 6/21/68, address 1197 Berlin Johannestal, Südost Allee 218, and Gaudian, Christian, DOB 10/17/68, address 1115 Berlin Buch, Wolfgang-Heinz-Str. 50, through border guards on duty in the area approximately 300 meters east of Straße 16."

The report continued: "The perpetrators scaled the Wall without the help of equipment and without being seen, and in the process set off the border fence alarm five meters away at 11 : 39 p. m. Units of the border guard deployed 200 meters eastward and 300 meters westward, at Straße 16 and

Photo of Border Guard Captain Karl-Heinz B., nicknamed "Kippe", which appeared around the world on April 9, 1989. The day before he had prevented the escape of two 27-year-old men at the Chauseestraße checkpoint (Berliner Morgenpost, Jan. 3, 1993.

„Kippe" – das Gesicht aus dem Alptraum

Im April '89 scheiterte ihre Flucht: Was Bert G. und Michael B. erlitten

Sie nennen ihn „Kippe", haben ihn bisher nur einmal im Leben gesehen. Es war vor knapp vier Jahren, am 8. April 1989. Damals, morgens um halb zehn, wollten ein Lanzestädtisches Überging Chaussestraße vom Mitte in den Westen nach Wedding fliehen. Sie scheiterten.

An jenem Sonnabend zerstörte „Kippe" als Hauptmann der DDR-Grenztruppen die Träume der beiden Ost-Berliner Bert G. und Michael B.: mit einem gezielten Pistolenschuß, an beleben kurz unmittelbar vor der beiden Grenzbarrieren. Sein Foto-Zigarette im Mund, Pistole im Anschlag – ging um die Welt.

Jetzt sieht das Flüchtlingen ein Wiedersehen mit „Kippe" unter anderen Vorzeichen bevor – vor Gericht. Die Staatsanwaltschaft beim Kammergericht, Arbeitsgruppe Regierungskriminalität, hat gegen den 49 Jahre alten Ex-Hauptmann Karl-Heinz B. Anklage erhoben wegen des Verdachts des versuchten Totschlags.

Nach den Angaben von Justizsprecherin Uta Fölster soll den Angeschuldigten „vorgeworfen, „nach einem Warnruf gezielt aus fünf bis sieben Meter Entfernung" auf einen der Flüchtlinge einen Schuß abgegeben zu haben.

Auf des Schicksals Schneide: Michael B. und Bert G. dieser Tage am früheren Kontrollpunkt, wo „Kippe" sie ins Visier nahm. *Fotos: Koal (2)*

nierten mit Hanteln und anderen „muskulösen" Gerätschaften.

Als ihre Flucht beschlossene Sache war, absolvierten sie auf einem Sportplatz in Friedrichshain ein Intensivtraining, Bert G.: „Wir liefen täglich mehrere Runden, übten Hürdenlauf, stoppten die Zeit. Den Übergang Chaussestraße hatten wir uns angeschaut. Im Spurt brauchen wir 14 Sekunden, hatten wir ausgerechnet. Das war so schnelle."

Ihre Bräute und die Kinder wollten sie nach geglückter Flucht auf dem Wege der Familien-Zusammenführung nachholen.

Am 8. April 1989 liefen sich die beiden Freunde mit einem Taxi bis kurz vor den Kontrollpunkt Chaussestraße fahren, ins nahe gelegene „Stadion der Weltjugend" drehten sie noch einige Runden, um sich warmzulaufen. „Bei dem regen Berufsverkehr glaubten wir davon aus, daß auf uns nicht geschossen würde. Unsere Chancen sahen wir 50 zu 50", sagt Michael B.

„Als wir die erste Barriere der Pkw-Slalomstrecke übersprun-

. . . Grenztruppen-Hauptmann Karl-Heinz B. („Kippe") zielt auf Bert und drückt ab . . .

ben. Laut Anklage habe der Beschuldigte „in Kauf genommen, daß der Schuß tödliche Folgen haben" könne. Ein Termin für die Hauptverhandlung ist noch nicht anberaumt.

Die Flucht vom Frühjahr 1989 hatten die heute 31jährigen Kraftsportler schon Wochen vorher geplant. „Aus unserem Bekanntenkreis waren fast alle schon im Westen. Wir waren mit unseren Verlobten die letzten. Da war klar – wir hauen auch ab", erinnert sich die beiden.

Obwohl die Fotos von ihrer Flucht millionenfach abgedruckt und von zahlreichen Fernsehstationen ausgestrahlt worden sind, blieb ihre Identität lange in der Öffentlichkeit unbekannt. Die Berliner Morgenpost sprach jetzt erstmals mit den beiden Männern – über ihre Motive, ihre Inhaftierung und ihr Leben vor und nach der Wende.

Bert G. wie sein Fluchtkamerad Jahrgang 1961, war vor vier Jahren Kellner im „Haus des Lehrers" am Alex, wohnte in Friedrichshain. Ein paar Straßen weiter, in Lichtenberg, lebte Michael B. Er arbeitete damals beim DDR-Fernsehen in Adlershof als Dekorations-Monteur. Beide haben je zwei damaligen Bräute 1989 geheiratet, jedes Paar hat ein Kind.

Bert und Michael eine nicht „nur die Abneigung gegenüber dem in der DDR praktizierten „Sozialismus", sie waren auch begeisterte Kraftsportler. In ihren Wohnungen richteten beide ein Zimmer als Fitneßraum ein, trai-

gen, rief ein Posten ,Halt! Stehenbleiben!'. Es gab Alarm, Sirenen heulten auf. Wir sprinteten auf die zweite Barriere zu, und als ,Kippe' in den Weg, rief ebenfalls ,Stehenbleiben!' und ,feuerte!", erinnert sich Bert G.

„Ich sah das Mündungsfeuer aufblitzen. Er hätte mich eigentlich mitten zwischen die Augen treffen müssen. Es ist ein Wunder, daß ich lebe. Die Kugel heulte an meinem Kopf vorbei, pfiff ein", sagt G.

Die beiden Flüchtlinge blieben wie versteinert stehen, wurden überwältigt. Nach Verhören in der Grenzkaserne kam Bert in die Stasi-U-Haft nach Pankow gebracht. Mitte Juli verurteilte das dortige Stadtbezirksgericht Bert G. zu 22, Michael B. zu 20 Monaten Haft.

Danach kamen die damals 28jährigen in das Jugendgefängnis „Frohe Zukunft" nach Halle. Die Maueröffnung erlebten beide im Februar im Knast, sahen, wie die Menschen zu Tausenden durch dem Kontrollpunkt strömten, der ihnen fast zum Verhängnis geworden war. Am 13. bezeihungsweise 15. November 1989 kamen sie frei.

Michael B. lebt heute als Neueinsteller in Spandau, Bert G. in Friedrichshain. Er ist Busfahrer bei der BVG. Und täglich fährt er mit demselben Gefühl ein Magen von Mitte nach Wedding zur Arbeit – über die Chaussestraße.

Lutz-Peter Naumann

. . . Bert muß aufgeben und sich auf den Boden werfen . . .

. . . zwei Grenzer halten Michael mit vorgehaltener Maschinenpistole vor Schach – der Fluchtversuch ist endgültig gescheitert. *Repros: BM(3)*

. . . aber heute als freie Menschen am gleichen Ort

Von Mitte nach Wedding: Michael B. und Bert G. spurten nach einmal über die Chaussestraße

Britzer Allee, immediately responded and carried out tactical border operations and apprehended both border runners."

A grotesque distortion of the facts, because Chris Gueffroy could not be "apprehended", as he died just after being struck by a hail of automatic weapons fire. On April 16th an unidentified man was found dead on the death strip — the last casualty of the Wall. According to a report prepared by the "Arbeitsgemeinschaft 13. August" published on August 9, 1996, 899 refugees perished since 1949 along the intra-German border,of which 753 died after August 13, 1961, with 239 of them dying at the Berlin Wall alone. In contrast, over 40,000 successful "barricade busters" were recorded in the period from 1961 to 1988.

Escape Route Prague

The year 1989 had begun, the year that would become the year of destiny for the GDR. Unquestioningly, large sectors of even the West German public still believed in the omnipresent slogan, "the tenth greatest industrial power in the world".

Events took their own course. Almost no one in the West noticed that relations between East Berlin and Moscow had cooled considerably. Following his visit to Magnetogorsk, where as a Young Communist he had spent several weeks in the thirties, Honecker privately made jokes about the food shortage in the Soviet Union. Politburo member Kurt Hager poked fun at Gorbachov's policy of perestroika, saying that just because one's neighbor was putting up new wallpaper, that didn't mean one had to install the same wallpaper in one's own apartment. In that same context, several Soviet newspapers, for example "Sputnik", were banned by the GDR authorities. The men in power were afraid that the paper ostensibly promoted anti-Party thinking in the GDR along the lines of the perestroika policy. In contrast to this laboriously camouflaged rejection of the Gorbachov policy, the new ideas of the Kremlin leader gained increasing acceptance, primarily among intellectuals, artists, and scientists.

In January 1989 the alarm bells rang in the SED command centers: on the anniversary of the death of Rosa Luxemburg and Karl Liebknecht, a day that was sacred to every Communist and a day when the entire Communist elite took part in a mourning procession, young people found a whole new way to "provoke": carrying placards with Rosa Luxemburg's dictum that "Freedom is always freedom to think differently", they tried to join in the procession marching toward the "Cemetary of the Socialists". The attempt was repulsed with rigorous force. With this, however, the Luxemburg quote did not fade away — in contrast, it was on everyone's lips.

This event in January was followed by an equally unusual occurance in March: for the first time, a group of 600 people seeking to emigrate protested in Leipzig against the withholding of their exit visas. At that time more than 750,000 applications for exit visas were on file with the authorities.

Then came May 7th, when another local election had been arranged. Once again, the SED regime believed that it had to present another mandate of almost 100 % to the people. A 98.85 % yes-vote was announced. The attempt at deception backfired: representatives of the increasingly bold opposition turned up at many voting stations to observe the evening's vote count. They compared the numbers reported in the voting districts with those later published officially — and in this way absurd falsifications were brought to light. The regime reacted by demanding that the Justice Department impose severe penalties against such "slanderers". As late as September 7, 1989, 80 people who had protested the election fasifications were arrested.

Further developments followed quickly: in early May the rumor raced through the GDR that Hungary was about to open its border with Austria. The inevitable came to pass: GDR residents traveled quite legally to Hungary as vacationers, and illegally crossed the "green border" as refugees. Oth-

During the fall of 1989 dramatic scenes occurred, particularly on the grounds of the West German Embassy in Prague. Czech security forces repeatedly attempted to prevent refugees from reaching the Embassy's extraterritorial grounds.

ers claimed political asylum at the West German Embassy. Overnight about 150 refugees had gathered there. The next miracle happened quickly: Hungary allowed 108 of them to leave for Austria. The embassy was almost immediately overrun again. A mass exodus began, and the embassy in Prague was inundated also, despite violent efforts by the Czech police to block the access to the embassy.

Events acquired an irresistable momentum. Approximately 3,000 "vacationers" in Hungary crossed into Austria over the green border, from which the barbed wire had long since been removed. On September 11, yet another miracle occurred: Hungary officially lifted the barricades. Within the span of three days, 15,000 GDR residents had poured over the border — legally. Meanwhile thousands camped in the rooms, hallways, and grounds of the embassy in Prague. On September 30, Foreign Minister Hans-Dietrich Genscher (FDP) and CDU Minister Rudolf Seiters arrived at the embassy. From the embassy's balcony, the Foreign Secretary announced to the refugees that they had been given permission to emigrate by the East German authorities. His words were greeted with deafening cheers.

With an eye toward the upcoming ceremonies celebrating the 40th anniversary of the founding of the German Democratic Republic, the regime announced that it was prepared to cooperate. As a face-saving gesture, the refugees were to be transported across East German territory. Their subsequent entry into the West would then officially be classified as "deportation". The first transport trains were assembled and reached West Germany without any problems. Within just a few days, however, the embassy in Prague was again overflowing. Once again trains were prepared. This time, though, the situation facing the East German authorities was somewhat more complicated. Along the tracks through East Germany, thousands of people waited for the chance to clamber on board the train. There was a riot in front of the Hauptbahnhof in Dresden between the police and those wanting to emigrate. To guard against more of the same, on October 3 the GDR announced the "temporary pass- and visa-free travel between the GDR and Czechoslovakia for the citizens of the GDR, effective immediately".

The holes had been stopped up again, although at a heavy cost in prestige, but the pressure grew inexorably. The demonstrations of October 7–8, on the occasion of the festivities surrounding the GDR's 40th anniversary, and the increasingly vigorous "Monday Marches" in Leipzig, Dresden, and other cities were signs of an unmistakeable barometric change. After Honecker was ousted on October 17, the new SED leader Egon Krenz promised on East German television that new travel laws would be drafted soon. Furthermore, the restrictions imposed on travel to Hungary and Czechoslovakia would be lifted.

Speculation about a release of steam from the overheated kettle that was the GDR did not lead anywhere, however. The demonstrations continued to grow — on October 23, there were 300,000 people in the streets of Leipzig. Once again the regime gave in: effective November 1, restrictions on travel to Czechoslovakia would be eased. Thousands of people promptly streamed into the neighboring country, and Bonn's embassy was once again filled to overflowing.

Now Prague was getting nervous: the Czech authorities feared a "rebound effect on their own population", and proposed a solution that hit their comrades in East Berlin right in the solar plexus: every refugee should be issued a document proclaiming their discharge from East German citizenship. Prague's wish was granted. In this way on November 4, 4,000 people were allowed to travel diectly from Czechoslovakia to West Germany. The Wall still stood, but since that November 4th, East Germany had become an open country. The numbers spoke for themselves: from November 4–9, the authorities in Bonn reported that 48,177 East Germans had traveled to West Germany via Czechoslovakia. Almost none of them came back.

Honecker Is Deposed

What was the regime's own view of the situation? The GDR press made it perfectly clear: accusatory headlines appeared, for example "Carefully Prepared Provocation Against the

GDR", "Silver Lining for Hungary", "Ice Cold Business Against GDR-Residents", and so forth. All the subversive forces of imperialism were lined up against the GDR, according to the published complaints. Nevertheless, proposals for a more refined judgement struggled to make themselves heard in the Politbüro. Voices were raised in favor of a more flexible policy. Under the leadership of Kurt Hager, reactionary forces immediately counterattacked: wait, until Erich Honecker returned. The State and Party leader was still recuperating from a gall bladder operation.

When Honecker reappeared on stage, he bore the marks of his illness: his gait was uncertain, and his speech awkward. The Party leader did not have much time for convalescence, because the date of the 40th anniversary celebration was drawing nearer.

On the evening of the festivities, 100,000 torchbearing members of the Freie Deutsche Jugend (Free German Youth) passed by the reviewing stands on which Gorbachov and the State and Party leaders of the Eastern Bloc had taken their places next to leading officials of the SED. What an insult to Honecker, however: it was not he but rather the VIP from Moscow who was the recipient of the FDJ's never-ending chants of "Gorbi, Gorbi". The same welcome had greeted Gorbachov earlier when he "pressed the flesh" among the East German crowds. His words, condensed into the catchy slogan "He who is late is punished by life", were soon on everyone's lips.

In Schloß Niederschonhäusen, Gorbachov's residence during his stay in Berlin, the Kremlin leader immediately met privately with Honecker. Nothing is known of the subjects discussed. Afterward a meeting of the SED-Politbüro was convened. During this meeting, the latent tensions between the SED regime and Gorbachov's perestroika policy came to the surface. Honecker painted a portrait of a blooming GDR, an indirect signal that his State did not require reforms in the Gorbachovian sense, because they had already been instituted. In his book "The Politbüro" (rororo), Günter Schabowski relates Gorbachov's reaction to Honecker's exposition: the Kremlin leader and his party listened without sayng a word, and then with a "tss" through their teeth they arose and left the chamber.

By then the decision had been reached by some members of the Politbüro to force Honecker's resignation, in order to spare the GDR further harm. Krenz and Schabowski, representing the "youth", and Alfred Neumann and Willi Stoph from the "old guard" were the chief conspirators, who now tried to win over other comrades to their plan.

Honecker's fate was to be decided at the Politburo meeting on October 17th. Shortly beforehand, Schabowsky had telephoned the Soviet Ambassador, who listened without saying a word, to inform him of the "rebels'" plans. The 21 members and five candidates who made up the Politburo gathered on that fateful Tuesday. As Honecker, after some introductory remarks, moved to get on to the day's business, he was interrupted by Stoph. The Advisory Council chairman suggested a change in the day's agenda: he moved that the first point of discussion be the dismissal of the General Secretary. Stonefaced, Honecker agreed — and the vote sealed his fate. Informing the 200 members of the SED central committee of the new leadership was only a matter of form. Honecker announced his resignation for reasons of health. In his resignation he announced his autocratic wish to see Egon Krenz appointed as his successor, a wish which was granted. Honecker had been in power for 18 years. Now the death-throes of the GDR began — not because of Honecker's exit, but in spite of it.

In West Germany there was widespread astonishment. Dreams of a reunification had always been considered a mirage, always in sight but completely out of reach. There were politicians who sought to dismiss any thought of reunification as the "mendacity of false hope". They pointed out that during the riots in Leipzig no one had spoken of reunification.

That was soon to change. The rallying cry "We Are The People!" would become after the Wall's collapse the cry "We Are One People!" A mass-movement "Democratic Revolution" was born, while the "Neues Forum" tried unceasingly to gain government recognition. In response the GDR authorities formed a new social-democratic party, under the initials SDP. It later turned out that the leaders of both the SDP as well as the "Democratic Revolution" were long-time Stasi informants.

Was The Stasi in the Dark?

Since early 1989 signs of widespread dissatisfaction had become increasingly apparent throughout the GDR: the Monday Marches in Leipzig drew ever-increasing numbers of participants, hundreds of thousands of people had applied for exit visas, and the West German embassies in Prague and Budapest were flooded with refugees. Inevitably, the question arose how it could have come to pass that the Stasi, widely considered all-powerful and all-knowing, was caught so completely off guard by this development. Were they restrained by a government that could not bring itself to close the borders to Hungary and thus be cut off from the USSR? Or were the Politburo's hands tied by Gorbachov's stated policy that the Soviet Union would keep its troops in their barracks in the event of any violent clashes in the GDR?

With regard to how far the widespread tentacles of the Stasi actully reached, apparently not even Honecker himself was in possession of all the facts. In the above-mentioned interview with the journalists Andert and Herzberg, he maintained that he had always believed that the Stasi personnel, including members of the "Felix Dzierzynski" regiment, numbered approximately 35,000. Honecker claimed to be completely surprised when he was informed of the actual numbers, namely 85,000 headquarters employees and over 100,000 "IM's". The astonished journalists asked Honecker about his personal responsibility as State and Party leader. Honecker answered with disarming frankness: "Please know, that today it is the fashion to assign all responsibility to the top. I am completely prepared to accept that responsibility. However, despite all the different opinions, announcements, and rumors, one thing is certain: we had a collective leadership in the Party. We had a collective leadership in the nation, and we had a collective leadership in the area of defense and security. Naturally I had those individual duties, but when one draws from that the conclusion that I therefore had to know everything, then one has the wrong impression of the man who stood at the top."

Even Honecker's "real" numbers showed that he was poorly informed. In the new "Dictionary of State Security", published in August 1996 by the Gauck Office (Ch. Links Verlag), which was formerly a top secret file limited to 400 copies, the number of "IM's" was put at around 600,000, of whom 174,000 were still active at the end.

This Stasi filled kilometers of shelves with unbelievably detailed files — everything that had been reported by its approximately 600,000 informants had been archived. The English philosopher and statesman Francis Bacon said that "Knowledge is power", but at the end for the Stasi it became more a matter of "He who knows too much knows nothing".

Nevertheless, the Stasi did prove itself capable of passing judgment on the explosive situation in the GDR — if only two months before the Wall's collapse. In a top secret situation report filed September 9, 1989 under "MfS, ZAIG, 0/225", the reasons for the increasing disenchantment among the population, as demonstrated by the increasing number of exit visa applications and the increasing outflow of refugees through "Socialist Brotherlands", were analyzed as follows:
– Influence of the ideological diversions of the enemy, particularly via the mass media,
– Negative influences of visitor traffic from East to West as well as West to East

– Dissatisfaction over the food supply situation
– Restricted travel opportunities within the GDR and abroad
– Disagreement with the media policies of the GDR

All these abbreviated reasons were then explained in great detail. The privileged few who were allowed to read this report, however, failed to react. And when the top leadership finally did manage to pass measures guaranteeing freer travel for the population, and to begin the wholesale dismantling of the Wall, their measures seemed more like the unexpected consequences of an industrial accident than a carefully considered plan intended to depressurize the situation.

If there were any doubts during the whole deterioration of the internal political situation about whether the supposedly omniscient Stasi had grasped the gravity of the situation, by the beginning of November they were laid to rest. Two days before the Wall fell — from the historical perspective, far too late — Erich Mielke, the State Security Minister, circulated among the small circle at the top an apprehensive report on the threatening circumstances. In the top secret document "MfS, ZAIG, Nr. 496/89", he confirmed the rapid increase in politically-motivated meetings organized by religious institutions and the sharply higher numbers participating in open-air demonstrations. For the week of October 30-November 5, he reported that "According to reports at hand, more than 1.35 million people participated in over 210 demonstrations, information meetings and other events". On November 4th alone, over one million people marched in the demonstration on Berlin's Alexanderplatz.

In the previous week, according to Mielke's report, a mere 540,000 participants had been observed taking part in 145 similar events.

The Border Disappears

"We did not realize, that the collapse of the Wall spelled the beginning of the end of the Republic. On the contrary, we expected a period of stabilization, which is in fact what occurred." That was the subsequent comment of Günter Schabowski, who under Honecker's successor Egon Krenz was the SED Politburo member responsible for press questions.

The new leadership was under tremendous pressure and had to propose something. In the future, all stipulations attached to applications for "permanent journeys abroad" were to be abolished. That meant that the hundreds of thousands of people who had applied to leave the GDR were to receive permission to emigrate. At the same time "private journeys" would now be made possible as well. That regulation was accompanied by the following sentence: "Applications for private journeys abroad can now be made without the provision of prerequisites (Reasons for travel and family relationships)". The immediate distribution of permits was promised, and moreover "reasons for disapproval would apply only in exceptional cases". One requirement for "private travel", however, was the possession of a passport—which only a small fraction of the population had. Getting a passport took up to six weeks, and thus the regime hoped to buy a little time.

The next hours would show that this calculation was incorrect. On the contrary—following a chain of mistakes it would lead directly to the opening of the Wall. When Schabowski was assigned to announce the new regulations at an international press conference, he was caught in his own lack of knowledge, as he had not been made privy to all the details in advance. Just before 7 p.m., as the press conference was drawing to a close, he was asked when the new regulations would be put into effect. Schabowski appeared flustered by the question, leafed through his notes, hesitated for a few seconds, during which it occurred to him in a flash that the Soviets had to be consulted before any changes in the greater

Berlin personal travel rules, and finally blurted "immediately" and "at once". It was a complete sensation. There was to be sure some mention of a deferment until 4 a. m. on November 4th, but even the "Camera of Current Events" show on East German television paid the postponement no heed. Shortly thereafter Hans-Joachim Friedrichs appeared on the ARD's "Tagesschau" ("Today Show") and announced: "The GDR has announced that effective immediately its borders are open to all. Travel to the West is now free and clear."

Schabowski later made the comment that "No one could undo the damage done in that moment". An avalanche had been set in motion. In apartments, on the streets, in bars, in stores — everywhere was heard the question: "Have you heard? They say the borders are open ..." At first there was astonished disbelief, and then thousands started moving. By foot, by bicycle or in their Trabis and Wartburgs, they went. The border guards were taken by complete surprise by the tidal wave of people crowding the crossing points. In confusion they called their headquarters. Even there word had to come from "above". After a quarter hour of complete chaos everything was decided: All persons would be allowed to pass, provided they could show legitimate personal identification.

Beyond the crossing points, on the West Berlin side, hundreds of people alarmed by the sensational reports had already gathered. The scenes that followed were shown on television around the world: complete strangers from East and West fell into each other's arms in tears, champagne corks popped, and West Germans pounded on the roofs of the visiting Trabis and Wartburgs in excitement. The word most often heard to describe the joyous amazement of those hours was a long-drawn-out "Waahnsinn!" ("Insanity!"). The divided city became the scene of a gigantic festival of joy. East German cars drove up and down the Kurfürstendamm. Their occupants were spontaneously invited into the apartments of West Berliners.

The night of November 9–10, 1989. The picture speaks for itself.

The border crossing at Invalidenstraße on that historic night: tears of joy, champagne, and continuous applause.

West Berlin's incumbent Mayor Walter Momper (SPD) coined the phrase that made headlines: "Today we Germans are the happiest people in the world." And Willy Brandt, who had occupied that office until 1966, said, "What belongs together must now grow together." Chancellor Helmut Kohl had just arrived in Warsaw when he received the first vague reports of the opening. His staff labored to confirm the reports during the hours that followed. Then the Polish side was asked to excuse the hasty conclusion of the visit. Because his West German Air Force plane was not allowed to land in Berlin, he first flew to Hamburg, where an American military aircraft was waiting. He arrived just in time for a rally in front of the Schöneberger Rathaus.

In those early evening hours, Gunter Schabowski, whose press conference just hours before had been the cause of this avalanche, stood at the crosspoint on Heinrich Heine Straße, between the precincts of Kreuzberg and Mitte. Months later he revealed what was on his mind during those moments: "Now the GDR's time is up."

It was not yet up. Practically all the East Berliners returned, most of them to return the next day to take in the "Showcase of the West" by daylight. With them came tens of thousands who had not managed or dared to make the visit on November 9th. Incredible scenes occurred all along the intra-German border. Seemingly endless lines of cars waited at the crossing points for the chance to drive into the West.

The traffic was one-way until December 23, when West Berliners were able to visit the eastern parts of the city: they had only to show their personal identification at the makeshift checkpoints.

By midmorning on November 10th, the high councils of the SED had not yet regained their composure. In the Central Committee's breakfast room, small groups gathered to discuss whose failure should be blamed for the disaster of the night before. If anyone in the circle of senior office-holders believed that the population would now be satisfied with the

The morning of November 10, 1989: Every car from the East was still being welcomed by enthusiastic West Berliners at the Bornholmer Brücke.

November 11, 1989: throngs of East German citizens waiting in front of the Sparkasse (Savings Bank) at the Kottbusser Tor in Kreuzberg for their 100 D-marks in "Welcome Money".

Everybody to the Brandenburger Tor! Seeing it with one's own eyes was the only way to be sure it was all true.

new status quo, he was soon disappointed. Calls for reunification grew ever louder, and soon a catchy slogan was making the rounds: "If the D-mark comes, then here we sit, if it doesn't, we'll go to it".

What Happened to the Wall?

"Wall woodpeckers" soon went to work on the symbol of separation with their hammers. Tirelessly they knocked off pieces large and small, preferably brightly painted ones, to sell as souvenirs.

Soon the demolition was in full swing. First all the old crossing points were reopened. Each time hundreds of enthusiastic onlookers would gather, bursting into applause every time a crane hoisted yet another segment aloft. There was a lot of work ahead of the demolition squads: 106 running kilometers of concrete, in nearby rural areas 127.5 kilometers of alarm-equipped and electrified fence, 20 earthen bunkers, 302 watchtowers and countless kilometers of wire fences all had to be torn down.

Entire segments were crushed by machines and made use of as fill for the construction of new streets between new states and old.

Interested parties from all over the world quickly asked

It was not enough that the Wall was now porous. It had to go!

The "Border organs" defended themselves for the last time against the assault on their "Peace Border" with a limp stream from their water cannon atop the Wall in front of the Brandenburger Tor. The dikes, however, had long since broken.

The first "Wall Woodpeckers" at work.

GDR officials tried one more time to regulate the flow of travelers by means of six-month visas ...

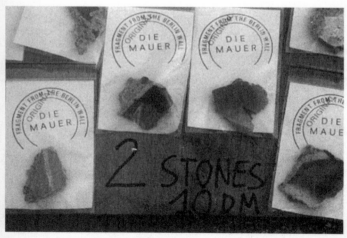

... meanwhile the Wall had long since become a souvenir.

The official dedication of the new thoroughfare through the Wall in front of the Brandenburger Tor, the most famous symbol in German history. Rudolf Seiters, Erhard Krack, the former Mayor of East Berlin, and Hans Dietrich Genscher can be seen next to Chancellor Kohl, incumbent Mayor Momper, and East German head of state Modrow.

whether they might acquire mementos before the whole Wall was pulverized in this way. A kind of "Wall-Export" arose, where for example a master baker from Badischen bought two support columns for 80,000 D-marks. A Berlin dentist of Polish extraction, Ludwig Wasecki, acquired 52 segments, which he had installed on a piece of land in Breslau (Wroclaw). In the summer of 1990, a number of segments were auctioned off in Monte Carlo — for 20–30,000 D-marks apiece. Among the buyers was a granddaughter of Winston Churchill, a member of the cognac-dynasty Hennessy family, and the wife of an Italian publisher.

The sale of Wall segments brought in around two million marks, which Germany spent to help improve basic public health in the ex-GDR. The pulverized remnants of the Wall were sold for 20 D-marks per ton. Even the fire-proof zinc-plated steel fences which had stood in the foreground of the death strip were sold. Pieces measuring 3 x 1 and 3 x 1.5 meters were popular materials with which to enclose kitchen gardens, chicken coops and animal pens.

Not all the pieces of the Wall were sold, however, but rather some were given as gifts of honor. The City of Berlin, for example, presented former U. S. President Ronald Reagan with an entire segment. Reagan's successor George Bush, who was the first Western head of state to support German reunification, was also honored in this way. Other pieces went to the Pope, to museums in London and Israel, the UNO in Geneva, and the cities of Los Angeles, Prague, and Riga. Even the Moscow city government wanted such a gift. In South Korea a segment was mounted directly on the border with communist North Korea.

Seven years after the historic event, there are only three places in Berlin where complete sections of the Wall are still to be found: on Bernauer Straße, Niederkirchnerstraße, and the East-Side-Gallery. They are threatened by decay — a 1996 restoration effort faltered due to money shortages, squabbles over control, but also disinterest on the part of the public. Discussions in late 1996 on whether the entire former extent of the Wall, with its deeply embedded expanses of steel and concrete, should be marked for future generations came to naught. A number of voices were raised in protest.

The well-known civil-rights activist Bärbel Bohley, artist and founding member of the "Neues Forum" warned against forgetting: Berlin needed a "Foundation for its Conscience", because many people had already begun to forget the true value of freedom and how gravely it was threatened over the course of many years. Wolfgang Templin, another civil-rights activist, spoke up lest the "sands of time unfeelingly bury those who witnessed the East German struggle". The East German SPD politician offerred this viewpoint: "It may very well be true that the Wall was torn down, even in a destructive rage. Everyone wanted to be rid of the imprisoning Wall, that stone document of freshly-defeated oppression and separation. Yet what was at the time an act of emancipation will gradually become an act of historical suppression if the last pieces of the Wall are not preserved".

Where The GDR Can Still Be Seen

Two years after the Wall was built, an audacious undertaking began in its shadow, right at Checkpoint Charlie on Friedrichstraße: an exhibit, which quickly became a museum. In many ways charmingly improvised, it was not mounted by professionals and designers, but rather by men and women who expressed themselves in words, writings, and deeds against Communist injustice. In the beginning it made its temporary home in a three-room apartment and a former café. The founder was Rainer Hildebrandt, who had been involved in the anti-Hitler resistance and, after the the national-socialist dictatorship had been replaced by the communist, founded the anti-communist "Kampfgruppe gegen Unmenschlichkeit" ("Action Group Against Inhumanity"). The exhibit opened on June 14, 1963. The "Haus on Checkpoint Charlie" subsequently became known as the "Wall-Museum".

Gradually the number of exhibits grew, and with them the number of rooms. Every work exhibited paid witness to the inhuman division of a city which had achieved a history dating back more than 750 years. There one can still see today pieces of the hot air balloon in which the two families flew from Thuringia to Bavaria. In addition there is a diverse collection of escape vehicles which were used to smash through the border, one of them riddled with bullet holes. Also on display is the home-made mini-submarine in which Bernd Böttger escaped across the North Sea to Denmark in 1984. A family's courageous escape attempt by "cablecar" from the roof of the "Haus der Ministerien"—only a few hundred yards from the Musuem—is recreated. Also among the exhi-

The "Haus am Checkpoint Charlie", founded by Rainer Hildebrandt (center), documents the history of Berlin's division with all its political and (in)human facets.

bitions is one of the self-firing-weapons, the cause of so many escape tragedies — altogether an instructive picture of the technology of the German separation. Additionally, later there were special exhibits such as "Painters Interpret the Wall", "Berlin — from City on the Front to Europe's Bridge" and "From Gandhi to Walesa — Nonviolent Struggle for Human Rights". This non-violent struggle was and is a particular concern of the museum's founder. Hildebrandt warned early not to see those border soldiers as monsters, but to "see through the uniforms". There were also repeated appeals to the border guards not to aim their shots at refugees. Soldiers who had fled were invited to speak at the museum.

"It was essential to document the injustice" said Hildebrandt about his motive for founding the museum. Even in the coldest days of the Cold War the leadership of the museum wanted to present an objective picture of the circumstances and to report unpolemically on human rights abuses.

The founder's idea caught on: even in 1985, over seven million people had already visited the museum. The "Haus am Checkpoint Charlie" was still standing after the Wall's collapse. There are regular lectures, and films are shown. The museum's leadership was also active in the field of journalism, and in 1982 founded the "Verlag Haus am Checkpoint Charlie", whose archives include a collection of over 80,000 photos of the time of German separation.

Another place of remembrance was established some distance north of the Mauer-Museum: in the new building "Quartier 200" by the architect Jürgen Engel, the southern third of the building is pierced through by a cylindrical rotunda open to the sky. It is the site of an open-air exhibit featuring pieces of the old barricades.

Still more reminders of the time of separation can be seen in the Alliierten-Museum (Museum of the Allies), which was founded at Clayallee 135 after the withdrawal of the Allies. Among the exhibits is the U. S. helicopter "Spirit of Steinstücken", which regularly flew to the enclave belonging to the West Berlin region of Zehlendorf. Also on view is one of the tanks which stood muzzle to muzzle during the dramatic confrontation between Soviet and American tanks at Checkpoint Charlie in 1961. The British donated their helicopter "Chipmunk", in which for many years they flew reconnaissance missions over East Berlin territory, as well as an armored "Scoutcar", which they employed during patrol missions through the Soviet sector.

In 1996 a memorial was dedicated at the former border crossing point Marienborn in Sachsen-Anhalt. The 35-hectare area was once a maze of walls, watchtowers, tank traps and warning signs. Every automobile traveller who wanted to drive from Helmstedt to Berlin on the A2 was stopped here. Today visitors can take in the more than three kilometers of underground passageways, have the security- and and supervision installations explained to them, and have a look at the cockpit of the watchtower with its green-painted control board for the barricades, turnpikes, and signal- and alarm systems. From here at the touch of a button the border guards could cause a barricade to roll across the highway. It was designed not just to stop a vehicle from crashing through, but to destroy it in the process. Any truck of up to 50 tons which tried to crash through at speeds up to 80 kilometers per hour would be smashed to pieces by the impact with the barricade. The small passport control hut was also equipped with the very latest technology. Videocameras photographed every passport handed through the windows. Personal data and photos would then be transmitted to the staff building and there compared with the list of suspects issued by the Stasi. In addition there was a very unusual mortuary on the large grounds of border checkpoint Marienbad, in which the coffins used to transport the dead between East and West were inspected.

Two more memorials still remain along the former inner-German border. In Mödlareuth, on the Thuringian-Bavarian border, a 70-meter-long section of the Wall is maintained by both governments. On the edge of the Magdeburger Börde, in Hötensleben, the entire system of former barricades has been preserved over an area of 400 meters long by 100 meters deep. The site has been granted historic landmark status. The 2,600 residents of the village have a saying, "Whoever among Berliners wishes to see the Wall, must come to us in Hötensleben …"

"Growing Together" in Theory and Practice

What happened after the cheering died away? What became of the "growing together" of which Willy Brandt had spoken? "Yesterday in each other's arms, today on each other's nerves" ran the saucy cabaret "Die Distel" ("The Thistle") in East Berlin. A satirical exaggeration — but a hard kernel of truth remained which could not be explained away.

Seven years afterwards, mutual dissatisfaction was widespread, with complaints in the "new states" (the former East Germany) of arrogance and a "conqueror mentality" on the part of the "Wessis" (West Germans). The reality was that legions of know-it-alls had overrun the new states, along with hordes of carpetbaggers and swindlers. On the other hand, far too many "Wessis" believed that they were owed gratitude by the "Ossis" because of all their financial aid, estimated by the Rheinland-Westphalia Institute for Economic Research at one billion marks. One banal example: especially in Berlin, there is even today the expression "drüben" ("over there"). The German language still draws a distinction between East and West Germany. One travels "over there" when one goes from one to the other, and for many such a journey is like a trip to a foreign country. Supposedly there are still "West Berliners" who, years after the collapse of the Wall, still have to think where Köpenick is. Conversely, many "East Berliners" know almost nothing about the western parts of the city.

Unfortunately, it is all too true: millions of West Germans are more likely to travel to the Bahamas or the Maldives than the Saxon Schweiz or Mecklenburg's lake country. By the same token, Mallorca is a greater draw for many East Germans than is Bavaria or a boat trip down the Rhine.

Many East Germans do not like being reminded that back then they thought of the decades of separation as a period of sorrow. What is worse, a sort of GDR-nostalgia has arisen, and the SED-successor PDS party has achieved frankly incredible election results in some areas.

Those in the West must ask themselves, whether they have not perhaps been too hasty and self-centered in passing over all the things that had been achieved in East Germany in addition to the many years of modest living standards. Sharp tongues noted dryly that only the green right-turn arrows at GDR street intersections had found favor in West German eyes.

Fatal forgetfulness and crass misconceptions must be laid on both sides of the Elbe and the Wall. Is "capitalism" to blame for the collapse of wide sectors of East German industry? Who could have foreseen that the image of the "tenth largest industrial state in the World" would be revealed as nothing more than an unholy rumor, an industry which would collapse the minute it had to compete with the rest of the world?

Researchers from all the German lands went over the German "soul" with a fine-toothed comb in an effort to discover how yesterday's cheers could become today's universal complaints. In the new states people considered themselves to be "second class citizens", that was clear to all researchers. The overwhelming majority expressed fears of societal decline, while not even one tenth considered "freedom" to be the chief benefit of reunification. Only 40 % of the East German population chooses to remember the years of being led by the hand, of being spoken for, of having every aspect of one's life controlled by the GDR-regime.

Didn't some Germans in the western parts of the country experience the same phenomenon in 1945? Weren't there great numbers of people in the years after the war who were of the opinion that things "hadn't been all bad" under the Nazis, pointing out the autobahns and the allegedly complete absence of any kind of criminal behavior?

At times the East German criticism reached absurd heights. For example, surveys revealed that 30 % complained that the West had provided too little financial assistance. This moves the people in the former Eastern-bloc countries to sigh comments like, "If only we had the same problems as the Germans".

The complaint can surely be made that too few East Germans play important roles in unified Germany's political and economic life. West German selfishness must be ruled out as the cause, however. Because during the 40 years of division, the science of government was exclusively in the hands of the Communists. Independent thinkers stood in the shadows. After reunification there were simply not enough East Germans who — unburdened with political baggage — were in a position to exercise leadership. The last Ministerpräsident of the GDR Lothar de Maizière employed a medical analogy: "I am not one of those who was of the opinion in 1990 that everything would happen overnight. I did have the hope that in five years we would have finished treating the wound and could begin treating the scars. We are still probing around in the wound and thus making it difficult."

The seeds of hope, however, are still growing. A six year study by the Children's Development Studies Department of the Free University in Berlin revealed that the quality of life for students in the East and West was now virtually identical. To be sure, East German youths still frequently describe their Western counterparts "Provincial, overbearing, inconsiderate, and aggressive". Another positive sign can be found in a study by the the Institute of the German Economy in Cologne, according to which only 14 % of East German youth criticized the social market economy, fewer than in the West. According to the survey, only 1.7 % wanted to bring back Socialism.

From the youth we go to the elderly: the "Seniors Report 1994" of the Berlin-Brandenburg Social Science Research Institute found that the older citizens are generally satisfied with their new living conditions. According to the report 47 % of the 50–60 year-olds and 51 % of those over 60 were "Very Satisfied" or at least "Satisfied" with their situation.

The publicist Claus Jacobi undertook a lengthy research expedition. During his journey he engaged in countless conversations. In his book "Aufbruch zwischen Elbe und Oder" ("Revolution Between the Elbe and the Oder") (Ullstein) he makes the following point: "Unity is not nearly as bad as its reputation. There is little that does not improve with each passing day." On the fifth anniversary of the reunification, East Berlin film director and civil-rights activist Konrad Weiß came to a similar conclusion: "In the meantime the national unity has been achieved, as complete as any human labor can be, full of unsolved questions and problems. However, it would be childish to believe that a society in ruins and a country so mismanaged could in the space of five years be transformed overnight into a blooming landscape." And in another passage he writes: "The new elite which East Germany needs will come from the ranks of those students who began their schooling in the old GDR, but who grew up in reunited Germany."

Will it, as some skeptics believe, be at least 20 years before the Germans have found one another and "grown together"? Even such pessimistic estimates by reputable contemporaries are no cause for alarm. On all sides the consequences of the 40-year separation have clearly been underestimated. In this day and age millions of people on both sides of the Wall and the border zones have been affected differently and have been deeply influenced by their living conditions. Differences in mentality have evolved which cannot be overcome from one day to the next. Honesty toward oneself is urgently required on all sides. Patience is essential. The Valley of Complaints that is part of German geography should be abandoned because it is there (where else?) — in the matter of moaning and groaning — that in the judgment of many of our contemporaries the Germans are united as nowhere else.

Timeline

1944	Sep.12	USA, Soviet Union, and Great Britain agree in the "London Protocols" on occupation zones in Germany
1945	February	France joins the "London Protocols" as the fourth victorious power
	May 2	Berlin surrenders
	Jul. 4	Western powers occupy their sectors of Berlin
	Jul. 17	Potsdam Conference (July 17-Aug.2)
1948	Mar. 20	Soviet representatives quit the Allied Control Council
	Jun. 24	Blockade of Berlin begins, Allies begin Airlift
1949	May 12	Soviets end Berlin blockade after 322 days
	May 24	Federal Republic of Germany (West Germany) founded
	Oct. 7	German Democratic Republic (East Germany) founded
1952	May 26	Allies sign "Deutschlandvertrag" ("Treaty of Germany") granting West Germany significant sovereignty
		GDR leadership closes intra-German border, plans "Operation Chinese Wall", and cuts 3,910 telephone lines to West Berlin
1953	Jun. 17	Popular uprising in East Germany
1955	September	"Moskauer Vertrag" ("Treaty of Moscow") grants GDR greater autonomy
1956	Nov. 10	Khrushchev delivers ultimatum demanding Allied withdrawal from West Berlin

1961	Mar.29	Warsaw Pact rejects Ulbricht's blockade plans
	Jun. 15	Ulbricht: "No one has any intention of building a wall".
	Aug.5	Warsaw Pact approves "Operation Chinese Wall"
	Aug. 10	Konjev: "Nothing will happen to West Berlin"
	Aug. 13	At midnight Eastern section of Berlin closed off from Western section Konrad Adenauer announces necessary countersteps
	Aug. 15	First protests by Western powers. Construction of Wall begun at Acker-straße. NVA-soldier Conrad Schumann leaps across the barricades
	Aug. 19	U. S. Vice-President Lyndon B. Johnson and General Lucius Clay travel to Berlin
	Aug.20	U. S. military convoy rolls toward Berlin on Autobahn transit route
	Aug. 22	Adenauer comes to West Berlin Ida Seikmann dies attempting to escape
	Sep. 17	Adenauer loses parliamentary majority in national elections
	Oct. 25	U. S. and Soviet tanks confront each other at Checkpoint Charlie
1962	Aug. 17	Peter Fechter dies on the Wall
	Oct. 15	Cuba missile crisis begins (Oct.15–28)
1963	Jun. 26	U. S. President John F. Kennedy visits West Berlin
	Dec. 18	First entry-visa agreement
1966	March	Wall "modernized" (until 1971)
1970	Aug. 12	Chancellor Willy Brandt and Prime Minister Alexei Kosygin sign "Moskauer Vertrag" ("Moscow Accord")

1971	Sep. 3	The Four Powers sign "Berlin-Abkommen" ("Berlin Accords")
1972	May 17	West German Parliament ratifies the "Eastern Treaty Package"
	Jun. 3	"Berlin Accords" become effective
	Dec. 21	Grundlagenvertrag (Basic Treaty) between East and West Germany
1974	Mar. 14	Protocols signed establishing "Permanent Representatives" in Bonn and East Berlin
1975	Jul.30	KSZE summit meeting in Helsinki (Jul.30 – Aug.1)
1976	Dec. 21	ARD correspondent Loewe deported from GDR
1979	Mar. 3	Since 1964 through the "extraordinary efforts" of West Germany over 13,000 political prisoners are released early and leave the GDR
1983	Jun. 29	West Germany grants one billion mark credit to GDR
1987	Jun. 12	U. S. President Ronald Reagan visits West Berlin
	Sep. 5	1,000 members of the non-aligned peace movement gather in East Berlin for an unannounced demonstration; not broken up by the police
	Sep. 7	Honecker visits West Berlin
1988	Jan. 17	Over 100 members of the peace- and human rights movement arrested in East Berlin for appearing at the official Rosa Luxemburg Parade with signs saying "Freedom is always freedom to think differently"
	Nov. 18	German language edition of "Sputnik" banned in GDR
1989	Sep.10–11	Hungary allows all GDR-refugees to leave for the West

	Sep.19	With the "New Forum" an opposition group makes first application for official status
	Sep. 30	Czech Republic allows all GDR-refugees to leave
	Oct. 2	20,000 people demonstrate in Leipzig for reforms in the GDR
	Oct. 6–7	Celebration of 40th Anniversary of the GDR. Gorbachov in East Berlin
	Oct. 10	Honecker deposed; Egon Krenz named successor
	Nov. 4	One million people demonstrate for democracy in the GDR
	Nov. 7	GDR government unanimously resigns
	Nov. 9	Günter Schabowski announces liberalization of travel. Thousands cross the border
	Nov. 11	Wall is breached at Potsdamer Platz
	Dec. 22	Official celebration of opening of Brandenburger Tor as thoroughfare
	Dec. 23	First traffic passes through the Brandenburger Tor
1990	Jun. 22	"Checkpoint Charlie" demolished
	Oct. 3	GDR accepts West German Constitution

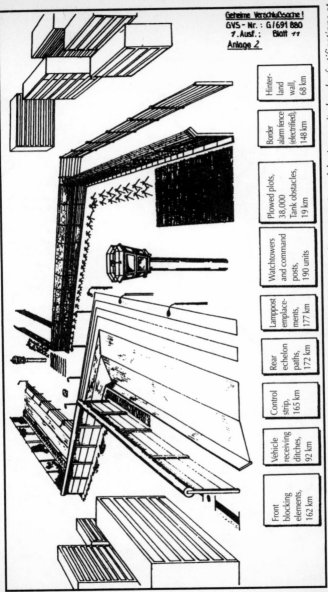

| Front blocking elements, 162 km | Vehicle receiving ditches, 92 km | Control strip, 165 km | Rear echelon paths, 172 km | Lamppost emplacements, 177 km | Watchtowers and command posts, 190 units | Plowed plots, 38,000 Tank obstacles, 19 km | Border alarm fence (electrified), 148 km | Hinterland wall, 68 km |

A drawing from the Ministry of State Security (Stasi), showing the typical construction of the inner-city border fortifications at the end of the 1970's. (West Berlin on the left, East Berlin on the right).

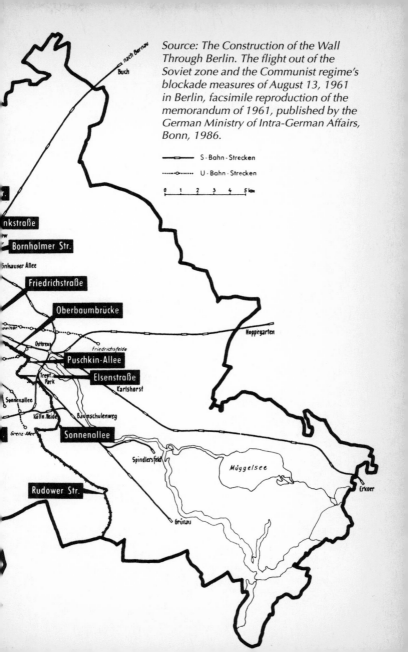

Source: The Construction of the Wall Through Berlin. The flight out of the Soviet zone and the Communist regime's blockade measures of August 13, 1961 in Berlin, facsimile reproduction of the memorandum of 1961, published by the German Ministry of Intra-German Affairs, Bonn, 1986.

S - Bahn - Strecken

U - Bahn - Strecken

0 1 2 3 4 5 km

Photo Inventory: